Have you ever wondered where God is in God even cares about you at all? Ever felt like someone threw the key away? Then Ruthie Jacobsen's book, "God Wants to Hear You Sing," is a must-read for you. In it she shares how we can find freedom like we've never known when we learn to sing in our midnight hour. We get God's total attention when we sing, sing, sing.

—DAVID RING, *Much-loved evangelistic speaker*

Anyone can sing their song on a clear day, but it takes divine courage to smile when we are in the midnight hours of life. Rodney Griffin is truly gifted by God to write songs that inspire the child of God to keep on keeping on. And the stories of lives changed by the message of the song are the greatest testament to that gift. The stories in this book will give challenge and encourage you to go to a new level of trust in our heavenly Father.

—MARK TRAMMELL, *Baritone, famed Mark Trammell Trio*

All the lives Rodney has touched… and his dad… and Bill West… are a tribute to the power of gospel music. The stories in this book will bring glory to God and courage to you.

—MAURICE TEMPLETON, *Former publisher,* Singing News Magazine

FREE MUSIC CD

Hear the songs you read about in the book!

Purchase the book, then visit our web site: www.GodWantsToHearYouSing.com,
and order the free music CD produced by Rodney Griffin and Greater Vision
to accompany this book. Order the CD from the website and we will ship it to you
within a few days for just the cost of shipping, and we will keep your
personal information strictly private.

Instead of the CD, if you would rather download the songs in MP3 format,
you may do so on the website — at no cost.

The book is great; accompanied by the music it is even better — and it's free!

GOD WANTS TO HEAR YOU

SING!

RUTHIE JACOBSEN *with* RODNEY GRIFFIN

Ruthie Jacobsen with Rodney Griffin

Cover & Content Design
Mark Bond for Bond Design, Inc.

Editors
Don Jacobsen and Richard Coffin

Cover photography copyright © iStockPhoto.com

Quotations from *The Clear Word,* copyright © 1994, Jack J. Blanco.
Used by permission.

ISBN   978-1-878951-08-3

TABLE OF CONTENTS

DEDICATION

As you read this book you'll meet Bill West. But it will not be a meeting with a trumpet fanfare. Bill is not a trumpet fanfare kind of guy. Bill is quiet but strong. He is gentle but passionate. When Bill shows up in the story he is a quality control foreman at a shipyard in Virginia, and a good one. But more, Bill is a genuine and steady representative of the Jesus he loves.

We have dedicated this book to Bill West because it was his influence in that shipyard that helped turn Jeff Griffin from a life of alcohol and bad choices into a brand new Christian. Indeed, for the past 33 years, Jeff has been an effective Christian pastor!

You see, Jeff Griffin is Rodney Griffin's dad, and no one had a greater influence in Rodney becoming a Christian, than his dad. Rodney, in turn, has used his gift as a musician to turn the hearts of millions of people all over the world toward the cross. I guess then, that makes Bill West, spiritually, "Grandpa Bill" to most of us.

So, Bill, because of your faithful witness and the debt all of us owe you, we gratefully dedicate this book to you. Without you, most of the stories included here probably would never have happened.

Ruthie Jacobsen
Rodney Griffin

FOREWORD

He was a man of great influence and wealth … and he was in shock. He had just received word that his sons and daughters were killed in a tragic accident. Still reeling from that tragedy, he found out that his family's means of living was wiped out in connection with the accident. Impoverished and deep in grief, he fell ill with a debilitating sickness. His closest friends expected him to throw in the towel and quit. But somehow, from deep inside, his faith emerged in an amazing prayer. And Job prayed: "The Lord gives and the Lord takes away. Blessed be the Name of the Lord."

Praising God is easy when life is easy. When the sun is shining, the family is happy, there's money in the bank, and you're feeling good, praise for our Father just naturally erupts from the lips of those who follow Jesus. What comes from our mouths when life is tough however, is what truly reveals our heart condition.

Family strife, loss of jobs, cancer, death; so often these are the daily companions for many, even for those who are Christians. When praise flows from our lives during these difficult times, we know that something truly supernatural has occurred. God has become bigger than our circumstances and the lifestyle of praise continues on uninterrupted.

My good friend, Ruthie Jacobsen, will show you how to live this overcoming life in this wonderful book. Inspiration matched with practical instruction will give you the tools to deal with any situation by staying focused on Jesus and worshiping Him in the midst of life.

This is a book to be prayed through. As you read, ask the Lord to deepen your faith through the life of praise. Pray that your eyes would be fixed on Jesus instead of your circumstances. This is a book to be sung through. You will be blessed and your walk with the Lord strengthened as you experience the power of singing your praises to God.

David Butts, Chairman
National Prayer Committee

About the Authors

 Ruthie Jacobsen was born on a 17-acre fruit farm in eastern Oregon, the ninth of ten children. Maybe that's why she still finds it difficult to pass up a roadside fruit stand that is selling Bing cherries. She graduated from Walla Walla University with an RN and a Masters in Education and spent most of her career in Nursing Education and Administration.

She's also known throughout her adopted hometown of Hiawassee, Georgia, for her knock-'em-dead brownies…and for tasting food off of strangers' plates — but that's a story for another time.

Ruthie studied both piano and organ and it was her deep love for music that eventually put her in touch with Rodney Griffin and the Greater Vision trio. It was Rodney's song, "God Wants to Hear You Sing!" on which the book would be based.

Ruthie hosted a weekly television program on Sky Angel Network for six years, has written numerous articles in nursing journals, and contributed to the book *Medication Errors*. She is Director of Prayer Ministries for her denomination in North America, a member of the National Prayer Committee, and a member of the Executive Committee of the Denominational Prayer Leaders' Network.

She and her husband, Don, are semi-retired in north Georgia, and have visited more than 120 countries.

RODNEY GRIFFIN, voted favorite song writer of the year for the past eleven years, was educated as a Biologist with an emphasis in horticulture and landscape design. (Now there's a good background for a song writer!) Rodney's first foray into the business world was at Newport-News Shipyard in Virginia where he worked in the construction of aircraft carriers and other naval vessels. (You can tell he's headed for a career in music, right?) It was during this time that his life-long desire to write gospel music began to blossom.

In 1993 Rodney joined Greater Vision which would become the most awarded trio in the history of gospel music. Much of the music the group sings comes from Rodney's prolific pen. He has written more than 350 songs, and writes for numerous other gospel music groups as well. The trio spends more than 200 nights each year in concert and is a frequent guest on the In Touch television ministry with Dr Charles Stanley and the Gaither Home-coming videos.

"The Lord is my strength and my song;

He has become my salvation.

He is my God and I will praise him.

He is my father's God and I will exalt him!"

(EXODUS 15:2, *The Clear Word*)

CHAPTER 1

God Wants to Hear You Sing – 1

"Fill us in the early morning hours with your love
so we can your praise throughout the day and
be glad the rest of our days."

(PSALM 90:14, *The Clear Word*)

SPRINGTIME IN THE SOUTH IS GLORIOUS! Miles and miles of dogwood, azaleas, blue skies, sunshine, and color emblazon the landscape everywhere. Anticipation had reached fever pitch at Beth's high school. This was the week of final exams, and everyone was ready for summer break.

Beth Burden, a fourteen year-old freshman, was studying hard for her final exams but not feeling up to par. Tuesday morning she woke up feeling sick to her stomach. "No time to be sick this near the end of school," she told herself half out loud. So she went to school, and by the afternoon felt better. Had she shaken it off—whatever it was? Was this just exam jitters?

But when Beth awoke the next morning she felt terrible. Dragging herself out of bed she ran to the bathroom and vomited. Now her parents were concerned, especially when her mom felt a knot in Beth's abdomen. Debbie, Beth's mother, went right to the phone to make an appointment with their family doctor.

Later in the day as Beth lay on the examination table in his office, the thoughts swirling through her mind were mainly concerns for another kind of exam. *I hope I can be finished here early, because I have an exam at school at 1 P.M.,* she was thinking. But Beth would miss the exam that day, as her doctor ordered extensive—and immediate—tests.

One of the first procedures was an ultrasound exam to determine the size and location of this ominous "knot." What they discovered was worse than they had imagined. Whatever it was, it stretched from Beth's pelvis to the bottom of her heart—nearly a foot long.

Beth's doctor scheduled an appointment with a surgeon, who would do more tests, but because this was Memorial Day weekend her appointment was set for the following Tuesday. The family physician said, "Just go home and try to have a great weekend. We'll see you in a few days. Try not to worry. We're going to help you with this, whatever it is."

Go home, and don't worry! Yeah, right! Beth thought. And the entire family was beginning to feel rising waves of panic by this time. Beth's concerns mounted. *What's wrong? Will I be OK? What are they going to find? What will they do to me?* She was in a daze. This was a heavy load for a fourteen year old to carry.

God responded to Beth and her family's anxiety and had already scheduled a providential appointment. It would prove to be a supernatural intervention for the Burden family. On Friday night they attended a concert of gospel songs from 6 P.M. until midnight, and there they were enveloped by songs of praise and worship. Some of their favorite groups were featured, and the Burden family was soaking it all up. It would be the perfect preparation for what lay ahead.

On Sunday night there was another gospel concert—this time it was Greater Vision, and even though they had heard them before and loved their music, that night there was something different—a new CD with songs they had never heard. They were blessed by this music and purchased the group's new CD, *Perfect Candidate*. They started playing it again and again. Debbie said, "We buy all their music, even if we already have the CDs or videos, because there will be someone who needs that music."

That weekend Beth spent a lot of time with relatives and caring friends. This also gave a big boost to her courage. Her grandparents drove hundreds of miles to be there, and another grandmother, who lived nearby, became a strong shoulder to lean on. As her family and friends gathered at their home, Beth's grandfather, a retired pastor, suggested that they gather in a circle around Beth and pray for her. They prayed, sang songs of praise, songs of faith, and laid hands on her as they had seen in Scripture (1 Timothy 4:14). Beth felt warm inside and very loved. Each one's tender prayer made her feel stronger. On Tuesday, the CT scans and other tests began. Surgery was scheduled for the following Monday.

After the pediatric oncologist studied the films, he called Beth's mother. He did not have good news. "We think this has possibly spread to her lungs, Debbie," he told her, "and we need more tests."

"This was a teary time," Beth remembers. "We cried, we prayed, and we faced the next tests, the very next day."

The medical staff seemed to have a sense of urgency. After the tests, they admitted Beth to the hospital on Wednesday afternoon for surgery on Thursday. "The reason for our haste," one doctor explained, "is that we thought this was a stage I cancer, but now with the results of the tests in we have to say we're dealing with something much more serious—she has stage IV.

The news was almost too sobering to comprehend. "We all knew this was the very worst thing we could hear," Beth would later say.

Just before the staff came to take her to surgery on Thursday morning, Beth's room was filled with all the people closest to her—her parents, her brother Dale, her sister Krysten, grandparents, and friends. They encircled her bed, and again they prayed and sang together. One of the songs was Beth's favorite, "Lord, I Need You." Beth tried to sing with them; it was the cry of her heart.

Beth reflects, "Just before they wheeled me out of the room, the thought hit me—*I might not come back!* Mom had to leave the room for a minute. I knew it was really hard for them too." But Beth smiled and accepted the kisses and goodbye pats from everyone.

Then began her long trip down the corridor and into the operating room. There the nurses greeted Beth warmly. Her pediatric oncologist, the surgeon she had come to trust, came over and spoke to her. "You're just going to sleep through this," he said. "We'll do all the work, and we'll see you a little later. Just think some happy thoughts now before you go to sleep."

Beth awoke in the recovery room, with Richard, one of the nurses, getting her ready to return to her room on the pediatric oncology unit. She was surprised to discover that it was all over. The welcoming committee waiting in her room couldn't believe that she was awake enough to be talking to Richard, as he teased her about keeping her arms and legs on the gurney as he wheeled her back to her room.

Now began the long thirteen days of recovery in the hospital. Beth's parents were by her side almost constantly. Beth's mother had a little ritual each morning that helped jumpstart the day. They began by listening to the entire *Perfect Candidate* CD. Each song was becoming indelibly impressed on their minds. The first song, "Use Us Jesus," became their prayer too.

"Use us, Jesus, Lord, here we are, ready to serve You, fill us, this hour.

Use us, Jesus, come near us as we pray, and do something special today."

(Words and Music by Rodney Griffin)

They prayed and sang with every song. What a change this kind of worship brought each morning!

Debbie later said, "I somehow felt that I was in a bubble of God's protection. We were all so dependent on God. One night, as I was walking out to my car, I felt overwhelmed with exhaustion and worry. There was such a deep sadness. But God reminded me of the words of the song, 'God Wants to Hear You Sing!' Beth would smile again, and she would sing! God always provided encouragement, and in so many different ways—through our church family, through friends, and through countless friends we knew were praying for us."

The Burden family asked God to make this a special time in their lives, and daily He showed them ways they were blessing others. Beth's father works for FedEx, in a building with about 40 others. When his coworkers heard about Beth's illness and the blow it was to the family, they all wanted to do something to help. Someone suggested that they put together a purse, something tangible that would tell the family that they were standing with them in their dark days. Imagine the surprise when Beth's parents opened an envelope from the FedEx staff, to find $600. It came at a time when it was really needed. The Burden family knew that God was surrounding them with His love.

Before the surgery, no one knew for sure if Beth's tumor was malignant, but they would know after surgery. When the pathology reports finally came back, they were saddened once more to discover that the large tumor was malignant. So after thirteen days in the hospital, Beth would face yet another challenge—chemotherapy—and this would prove to be worse than the surgery.

But seeing her friends brightened each day. They would tell Beth about the funny things that were happening at school or at their work. It still hurt to laugh, but Beth would grab a pillow and hug it to her tummy to keep from hurting too much. Visitors, other than immediate family, were never allowed to stay long, but it always helped to see them.

Beth spent only a few days at home after her surgery before she returned to the hospital to face five days of chemo. Then she was allowed to go home for two weeks to recover. Once again she had to return to the hospital for five more days of chemo. This took all the strength she could muster. The chemotherapy knocked her down, and it was a struggle to get back up. She lost all of her beautiful blond hair, and through her physical exhaustion and pain, Beth often fought back tears of frustration.

But the daily worship ritual became her foundation. This was the core of her hope and the one thing that never varied in her life. No matter what else was going on, she and her mom started their day with Greater Vision's CD, listening, singing, praying through each song. But they would need it often through the day as well.

The last song, "God Wants to Hear You Sing," became Beth's instructions from God. When her friends or family came to see her, they never left without hearing this song, and they sang and prayed together. That song became the signature song of Beth's survival. Because they heard it every day in the hospital, nurses, physicians, technicians—everyone within earshot—heard "their song." And people—scores of people—were somehow inspired by the encounter in Beth's room.

"Could I bring someone in to meet you?" a nurse asked one day. "There's a gentleman here whose grandson has leukemia, and this grandpa seems to have lost hope," she explained. "You all have enough hope to share." So the older man, looking for hope, entered Beth's room.

He was a pastor, but since his treasured grandson had become so ill, he found himself in a dry time in his life. He said, "This is affecting my ministry. It's so hard to accept." So Beth played the song for him.

"God wants to hear you sing, when the waves are crashing 'round you,

When the fiery darts surround you, when despair is all you see.

God wants to hear your voice, when the wisest man has spoken,

And says, 'Your circumstance is as hopeless as can be.'

That's when God wants to hear you sing."

The pastor smiled at Beth. He could see that she believed every word; it was her family's anchor. Then he listened, with tears coursing down his cheeks, as the trio sang:

"He loves to hear our praise on our cheerful days,

When the pleasant times outweigh the bad, by far.

But when suffering comes along, and we still sing Him songs,

That is when we bless the Father's heart."

(Words and Music by Rodney Griffin)

Light was dawning for the elderly pastor at last. After Beth and her family prayed for him, and he prayed for Beth and her family, he went back to his grandson's room. But somehow he didn't feel the same. He had found the hope he was seeking. Beth remembered the first song on the CD:

"Use us, Jesus, Lord here we are, ready to serve You, fill us this hour.

Use us, Jesus, come near as we pray, and do something special today."

(Words and Music by Rodney Griffin)

That had been the Burden family's prayer, and God had answered it. They didn't see their pastor friend until months later, when he recognized them in a restaurant and came over to their table. "You'll never know how much that song helped me," he said. "It was exactly what I needed. God used it to get me back on track, and I've been fine ever since. My ministry has been stronger, and even though our situation hasn't changed, I have. Thank you for sharing that wonderful song with me."

But Beth's ordeal was dragging on. After she somehow endured two series of chemo treatments and was facing her third, she confided to her mother, "Mom, I'm sorry, but I don't think I can do this again. It's awful, and I'm still weak from the last time." Debbie hugged her daughter, she knew how frail Beth had become, and they cried together. Then they listened to the CD, and their special song—"God Wants to Hear You Sing"—and headed for the hospital to begin yet another series of the dreaded treatments.

Their oncologist met them before Beth was taken to her room. He asked them to wait for a few minutes in the lobby while he made a quick phone call. When he returned, he had a big smile. "Beth, I've got some fantastic news for you. I've just talked with a friend of mine, another specialist who uses this particular drug therapy. I told her all about you and asked what she would advise. She said, 'I think she's had enough. She should be OK now.' So, go home, and come see me at the office in about a week. We'll set up a schedule for follow-up."

How do you say Thank You for a miracle of that magnitude?

Where is Beth today—two years later? She is finishing her junior year in high school, and she's feeling great. She still has regular checkups with her oncologist, but everyone is satisfied with her good health. Beth is having fun as she works part time at a Chick-fil-A, a fast-food restaurant not far from home. She's looking forward to having her own car soon.

When she sends her e-mail messages, Beth always adds a little tag on the end, a powerful verse of Scripture, that says "Be silent, and know that I am God!" (Psalm 46:10, *New Living Translation*)

Beth and a whole host of others have learned through her experience with cancer that God means just what He says when He urges us through His Word, to *sing.* And Beth will tell you, "That's what makes the difference."

" ... *Christ's love for us enables us not only to endure such things, but even to overcome them.*"

(Romans 8:37, *The Clear Word*)

CHAPTER 2

More Than Able

"It is not enough to have a song on our lips,
we must have a song in our hearts."

(Fanny Crosby)

MEET MARK LODENKAMP, a man who truly had a song in his heart. Now if you had known him as a child, you might not have expected to see the man he became. However, "with God all things are possible."

Mark grew up in a family that appeared respectable on the outside. His father, a successful engineer, provided well for his wife and children, but that's where the normal family picture stopped. When Mark was only 8 years old, his mother was diagnosed with breast cancer. As she became increasingly ill, Mark's father changed before their eyes, and they began to see a dark, sinister side. At first Mark thought he was the only one singled out for his father's sexual advances, but he would learn years later that his three siblings were also victims of their father's abuse.

As a child, Mark had no understanding of God or religion of any kind, for that matter. His only escapes for survival were when he would run out into his backyard to be alone. Throwing himself on the soft lawn, he would stare up into the clouds. After watching the clouds and trying to find meaning in his life, Mark would often somehow find peace.

On a sultry afternoon in September, when Mark was 10, his father arrived home early and was in an especially sullen mood. After washing up, he called for Mark to come into the bedroom. Sensing what might be in store, Mark didn't respond.

A few minutes later, his dad appeared in the living room and grabbed Mark by the arm. Mark was able to escape his grasp, pull away, and run out into the backyard. In the far corner of the lot, behind some shrubs, Mark flung himself onto the ground.

The grass seemed to embrace him and give him comfort. For a long time he lay there as he looked up at the sky, trying to make sense out of what his life had become. It was one of the many times Mark would take refuge in this place.

When his mother died, Mark's sisters were sent to live with relatives in New Jersey, and Mark and his brother went to live with friends in Missouri. This should have been a welcome respite, but as bizarre as it sounds, Mark's nightmare with abuse continued. A friend of the family picked up the pattern of molestation right where his father had left off.

Mark's brother became ill while they were living in Missouri, and when they discovered that he had leukemia, their father came to visit. Not long after that he told the children that he was remarrying and would be reuniting his family.

The new stepmother had four children of her own, so now they were a blended family of ten. They lived in one of the largest houses in the neighborhood, but behind those big doors lived a family trying to survive what Mark remembers as a hellish existence.

In his book, *Empowered Living*, Jim Hohnberger tells something of Mark's story.

"Mark says, 'It's hard for someone who has not grown up in an abusive household to understand, but the physical abuse, even the inappropriate physical intimacy, does not wound the spirit like the mental abuse that so often accompanies it. My father continued to molest me for many years. However, it was the cruelty of his comments that revealed the pathological evil that motivates someone who could have been respectable and accomplished much good in the world to degenerate into a heartless man with dark desires. I grew up never hearing the words 'I love you' except in the context of engaging in his animalistic activities.'"

When his younger brother died of leukemia, Mark got the blame. The emotional wounds that followed were excruciating. Mark knew the bitter tears of rejection and it seemed that no one cared. Even though he excelled in sports, no one from his family ever came to even one of his games.

There was the never-ending fear of ultimately being rejected. When some chore or activity didn't meet his father's or his stepmother's demands, Mark was threatened with being thrown out of the house. This kind of uncertainty always seemed to brew beneath the surface. His sister was kicked out of the house at an early age and maybe Mark's turn would be next. So as soon as he was able, Mark left and joined the Marine Corps. It was there that his life at last began to take a different turn.

Mark loved being a marine! He was physically fit, and academically he stood at the top of his class. He was invited to attend the United States Naval Academy on the basis of his leadership potential and superior academic record. He also distinguished himself by placing first in virtually every area of basic training.

Hohnberger shares with us Mark's comments: "'Some people struggle with the demands of military life, but I thrived. Compared to my struggle for survival at home, this was easy! There were clearly understood rules and expectations, as well as clear rewards for achievement, and compared with my father, the officers, while if not kind, were certainly fair.' When his training days ended, Mark found himself working as an air traffic controller in the beautiful state of Hawaii."

He was sure he at last had it made! He loved his job, had enough money for his needs, and was dating several extremely attractive women, including some models. He was enjoying all of life's pleasures, including illegal drugs, which grew well in that tropical paradise.

Mark knew that a number of his friends smoked marijuana, and Mark decided that it was just good business to sell to them, since he had to get his own supply anyway. But his downward spiral came to a halt with a providential motorcycle ride. His friend Dennis asked him to go on a ride with him, and because Mark had always loved motorcycles, he jumped at the chance.

What Dennis didn't tell him was that he was taking him to see his pastor. Mark was very uncomfortable sitting there in the pastor's office. He stared out the window and wondered when they would leave. But it became obvious that Dennis was *not* in a hurry. He seemed to have an endless supply of questions for this pastor. An hour went by, and Mark kept thinking, *Surely it can't be long now!*

After a while Mark found himself becoming part of the conversation. The amazing thing was that in their easy references about God, Mark again heard a voice that he seemed to recognize. It was that still, small voice which had so comforted him when he was a boy—the same voice that had lain dormant for years. Somehow now it was ringing loud and clear, and

Mark knew that this was the voice of his *true* Father.

Hohnberger again: "Mark says, 'When I was a child I didn't understand that it was God speaking to me, only that I was loved. Now I knew it had been God, and I turned to Him with my whole heart. We left five hours later, but I didn't leave alone. I had my Father with me. For me, Christianity has never been a religion. It's always been a relationship with the One I love—my Father.'"

Mark's life was transformed. He quit drinking, gave up drugs, and stopped every activity he thought might displease his Father. He still had a supply of marijuana on hand, though. What to do with it? He decided to sell it to another dealer and then give the profit as an offering at church! He later said, "I wouldn't do that now, and I'm sure my Father must have smiled. He takes us where we are and helps us in our stumbling steps." But Mark was growing spiritually. He was finding a God who was more than able to give him direction in every circumstance.

After his discharge from the Marine Corps, Mark moved to Wheaton, Illinois, where he made another decision that would dramatically change his life. In his neighborhood, he met an elderly woman who desperately needed someone to help her, so he volunteered. She became his friend, and he often took her on her errands.

While walking with her through the aisles of the supermarket and unaware that he was being watched, Mark was enjoying helping his friend find the items on her list. Maria, a beautiful young college student who was working part time as a checker in the supermarket, watched him. She was intrigued with the care he gave to the elderly woman. Finally, when they came to her counter and they exchanged pleasantries, Maria became even more impressed. All throughout the rest of her shift, she kept remembering Mark's laugh, his eyes, his quick smile. She hoped he would be back.

And Mark had some thoughts of his own. He remembered this beautiful young lady. She seemed intelligent and fun, and Mark soon found other items he needed from that market. As Mark and Maria visited, and later dated, they discovered that they had much in common. They both loved music—sacred and classical. They enjoyed sports, and most of all, they shared their deep love for their heavenly Father.

Maria's heart told her that Mark was *the* one for her, and Mark was totally smitten with Maria. Their wedding day was June 26, 1983. They began a wonderful Christian adventure together and have been blessed with four children—Rebekah, Esther, Rachel, and Jonathon.

We might expect that someone from a background as abusive and destructive as Mark's had been could hardly be expected to be an exemplary father—but he was. Mark's family activities always included family worship, music practice with the whole family, and singing together as a family. All four children became accomplished musicians and were invited to perform all across the country, including a concert with the von Trapp family singers, great-grandchildren of Captain von Trapp of the movie *The Sound of Music*.

Mark and Maria's family became a tightly-knit group in which the children thrived. Every week there was a family night that included all kinds of games—some funny, some highly competitive. Mark and Maria became close friends with their neighborhood banker, and one evening he stopped by for a visit. It was game night, and he was invited to stay and join in the fun. Mark's son Jonathon suggested that they play marbles. Mark tried to tell his son that they could find another game that might be more appropriate for a banker, but Jonathon just said, "He's a banker; he ought to be able to count them."

So everyone got down on the floor and played marbles. The banker said it made him feel like a kid again. He loved it, and the evening gave him a new understanding of what a healthy family could be. Having come from a dysfunctional family himself, Mark took the banker's observation as a personal testimony to God's transforming power. He is *more than able.*

For the Lodenkamp children, home was definitely the place to be. They spent long evenings reading aloud to each other. Summers were special with swimming, canoeing, and tubing down the river. They also enjoyed hiking, mountain climbing, boating, or biking on the trails near their home.

One day the second grade class, of which Jonathon was a part, was asked to name the most special place they had ever been. The children named their favorite vacation destinations and beaches—Disney World, Grand Canyon, a rodeo. … But when Jonathon, Mark's 8-year old son, was asked the same question, he surprised everyone with his answer: "My home." His parents were giving him what he needed and wanted most—themselves.

Jonathon would later say, "My father was not a large man, but he was a giant in my eyes. His name and his reputation made me a person of worth and value in other people's eyes, and the way they perceived him provided me with the respect of the community, long before I was old enough to earn it on my own."

The tranquility of life at their home near Green Bay, Wisconsin, where they later moved, was shattered for Mark and his family. One evening at a concert, he experienced excruciating pain. After numerous tests, they found that he had advanced cancer. Already it had spread to his bones. In working through the agony of the inevitable, Mark, Maria, and the children determined to continue their singing. They would keep on blessing others with their music and leave the future in God's capable hands.

The family ministered in many places during the long months of Mark's illness. Just a short time before his death, Mark was still doing what he loved—telling his story, sharing with others the truths he and his family had learned. He often told the children's story during a worship service, and during concerts he told of God's closeness with His children—even during difficult times.

During a phone visit only a few weeks before his death, Mark told me, "I find myself singing a lot these days, and really thinking about the words of the songs." One of his favorites was "Live Out Thy Life Within Me." Mark would go through every verse, and it became a conversation with God, a prayer from his heart. As Mark spoke on the phone, it was evident there was no self-pity, no complaining, no fear of pain or death. He, like Job, could say, "I *know* in whom I have believed." Mark knew that even though there would be an interruption in his life here on earth, he had the definite promise of life forever with Jesus and a joyous reunion with his precious family.

The final days were bittersweet for Mark, Maria, and the children. However, they never stopped singing; it seemed to give their dad new energy. Because he had for years been walking with Jesus, spending time at His feet, Mark could leave his family a supernatural legacy—a legacy of hope.

Until the day he died, Mark was able to share with others the assurance found in one of Rodney's songs. He knew his Father was more than able, and he had learned to trust Him.

More Than Able

"I used to live a life so sad and lonely, defeat was all that I could understand.
But then one day I prayed, 'Lord Jesus, save me!'
I placed it all into His loving hand.

"And found that He was more than able to enable me with overcoming power,
More than able to give victory again.
More than able to complete the task, no matter what the hour,
More than able to defeat this world of sin.

"If you struggle with a load that's much too hard to carry,
Give it up, and let the Master's work begin.
You'll find that He is more than able to give blessings from His table,
More than able to give victory again.

"My friend, can you relate to what we're sharing?
Are you amazed at what the Lord can do?
Have you ever given Him a load to carry,
And watched Him work, as He brought you safely through?

"And found that He is more than able to enable you with overcoming power,
More than able to give victory again.
More than able to complete the task, no matter what the hour,
More than able to defeat this world of sin.

"If you struggle with a load that's much too hard to carry,

Give it up and let the Master's work begin,

You'll find that He is more than able to give blessings from His table,

More than able to give victory again."

(Words and Music by Rodney Griffin)

Parts of the Mark Lodenkamp story have been taken from *Empowered Living* by Jim Hohnberger. Pacific Press Publishing Association. Used with permission.

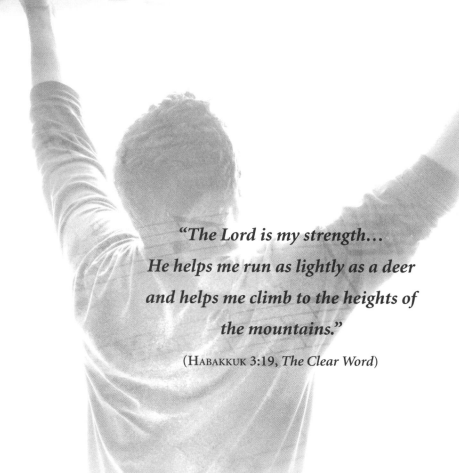

"*The Lord is my strength…*
He helps me run as lightly as a deer
and helps me climb to the heights of
the mountains."

(HABAKKUK 3:19, *The Clear Word*)

CHAPTER 3

A Spirit of Brokenness

"I will boast about Him for what He has done. Let all those
who are pressured and stressed stop and listen."

(Psalm 34:2, *The Clear Word*)

RODNEY GRIFFIN, VOTED SOUTHERN GOSPEL SONGWRITER OF THE YEAR
for nine years in a row and baritone for Greater Vision, recently went through a career-threatening crisis of his own. It was traumatic and prolonged.

In 2003 Rodney began to sense that his voice wasn't quite the same. Some of the notes that had always been easy for him to reach were now out of his range. He found himself straining to sing songs that he had sung all his life. Concerned, he went to his physician, who examined him and found a hemorrhaged nodule on his vocal chords. Dreaded diagnosis for a singer!

What does a professional musician do in the face of such a diagnosis? In public Rodney and the others in the trio got creative. On stage, he would lip-sync while a recorded version of his part was played. At the National Quartet Convention in Louisville, Kentucky, that year he was still unable to sing or even to speak, so when Greater Vision performed, his friend Mark Trammel sang his part from offstage, while Rodney mouthed the words on stage!

Plagued with questions about upcoming concerts, about his future, and about Greater Vision, Rodney's anxiety grew, yet he was under doctor's orders not to speak, so he couldn't even discuss matters with his family or colleagues. It was a dark night of the soul for Rodney. He could always continue to write Christian music, of course, but singing for the glory of God had become his passion. The thought of having to give up singing brought him indescribable anguish.

Finally, after the longest two months of his life, Rodney was permitted to sing again. His voice was no better, but no worse either. While he was searching to know God's will for his next step, a friend put him in touch with a throat specialist in Atlanta, Georgia. After a painful series of tests, Rodney was scheduled for surgery. This proved to be the miracle he needed.

As the soreness began to heal, Rodney began to hum and then sing. Within a few days he was able to sing at full volume with the same mellow tone that has thrilled countless audiences. When you hear him sing today "My Name Is Lazarus," you have no idea how close he came to becoming a stay-at-home songwriter.

After having gone through his valley of uncertainty, he shared with an audience in Pigeon Forge, Tennessee, this emotional journey in his life—and how it changed him. He described how he had wrestled through his potential tragedy, and had worked out with God his attitude about the future. He shared with the audience that night the following insights from his journey.

1. He acknowledged that God was in full control. As the weeks dragged on and he was unable to change his circumstances, Rodney was given an inner peace because he knew that his condition was not a surprise to God, who is the blessed Controller of all things.

2. Rodney grew to realize his total helplessness. In humility before his God, he was aware of his humanity and God's divinity. Daily he submitted his all to his Father. As he did so, his faith grew.

3. He came to the place where he could accept the fact of his inability to speak or sing, even though this had been his life. He came to the place of complete relinquishment of everything into God's hands. He said, "God, if I am never able to sing again, it's OK, and I'll not hold this against You."

It's like the complete submission and worship from the prophet Habakkuk, who also wrote a great hymn of faith, expressing that even though the worst might happen in an agrarian culture, he would still trust his God.

"Though the fig tree does not bud and
there are no grapes on the vines;
though the olive crop fails
and the fields produce no wheat;
though the sheep all die
and there are no cattle in the stalls,
I will still be joyful and sing.
I will rejoice in the Lord.
I will be glad that God is my Savior.""

(Habakkuk 3:17-19, The Clear Word)

As Rodney shared this chapter of his life at the concert in Pigeon Forge, he asked the audience of 1,200 to consider quietly the disappointments and detours in their own lives and to leave these with God. He invited each one to relinquish all, even if the outcome was not what they felt was best. God still reserves His best for those who leave the choice with Him.

In the audience that night was a father whose daughter had left home as a 14-year-old and had been gone for more than 20 years. The next morning this father told Rodney, "I've resented the way this has turned out. I've blamed God, because I knew He could have prevented it. I have held it against God. We've had no contact from our daughter. It's been anguish. But last night as you were speaking, I could see that I must let it go, give it to Him completely, and trust Him. So I gave all the hurt, everything to Him. I gave Him my daughter, and left her in His hands. I told Him, that even if things never turned out as I wanted, it would be OK. I would still trust Him, because He is God and my Father. And I told Him I'm not blaming Him anymore, just trusting. And now that I've given this to Him, I've experienced a peace that has been missing all these years. Thank you for sharing your story last night. It was just what I needed."

Rodney says, "Every writer has a favorite song that they've written, and "The Spirit of Brokenness" is my favorite. No, it's not the fastest, highest, or loudest, but it's my favorite. The reason is simple. . . . I'll always have a need to be broken. Wherever I am in my relationship with God, I'll always need to be closer. I'll never be finished. I'll always need a little bending here and there. And you know, He won't do anything with me until I give Him permission. He won't barge in. He's a perfect gentleman. That's why Rodney Griffin needs to hear this song.

"Our group's favorite evangelist is Bill Stafford, from Chattanooga, Tennessee. His every message seems to come back to one theme . . . brokenness. And we need to hear it. You see, in the gospel music world, we're constantly being told that we singers are great, talented, and the best of the best. And if we believe what we hear, we'll believe something false about ourselves. The truth is we're no different than anyone else. We're simply Christians. And every Christian has the same struggle—the Spirit versus the flesh. The flesh loves to hear about how good it is. It loves to think that it doesn't need help from God to attain goodness. And if you were honest, you'd admit that your flesh feels the same way. We don't like to be told what to do, by God or by anybody else. We all could use a little brokenness, whether we make our living on a stage on a construction site.

"After hearing so many Bill Stafford sermons on brokenness, I knew there had to be a song there. I finished the chorus but nothing more for six months. I couldn't get anywhere on the verses. All I knew was that I wanted the song to have the theme of humility all through it. I wanted to open up my heart and take the listener on a very personal journey of my spiritual walk with God, so I wrote it in the first person. You see, none of us stays on the spiritual mountaintop forever. This walk is oftentimes a struggle. And it's a battle that can only be won with a humble spirit, a spirit of brokenness." And, finally, the song was finished:

The Spirit of Brokenness

"I remember the night so long ago, the first time I called on Your name,
Empty and broken, ashamed of my sin, I asked if this sinner You'd save.
But the cares of life have darkened the light, and I feel like I'm drifting away—
So break me, mold me, cleanse me, then hold me. I want to be near you today.

"Lord, give me the spirit of brokenness,
Like You gave when I first called Your name

And replace all my pride with humility,

Lord, a broken, willing vessel I'll be.

"I never set out to drift into sin, my intentions are never to stray;

But my flesh is weak, and I'm so prone to fall, like a child I go my own way;

Till I hear Your cry, from deep down inside, saying, 'Go back to Calv'ry again,

Then you'll see My flesh opened, and My Spirit broken, then surely your drifting will end.

"Lord, give me the spirit of brokenness,

Like You gave when I first called Your name.

And replace all my pride with humility,

Lord, a broken, willing vessel I'll be."

(Words and Music by Rodney Griffin)

This song was especially meaningful to Valia, a member of Rodney's father's Northview Baptist Church, in Hillsboro, Ohio, when she first came back to the Lord. She had been living a life far from what she had chosen years before as a young Christian. But there was something in this song that spoke to her as nothing else could.

The power of a *song!*

Pastor Jeff Griffin, Rodney's father, tells of a member of his church who was having an especially bad day. Nothing seemed to be making sense, and he couldn't shake the sense of gloom that was settling over him. Finally in desperation, he put one of the Greater Vision CD's into the player in his car, and as he listened a change slowly came over him.

As the powerful words and music blessed his soul, things seemed to come into perspective, and he could see light at the end of the tunnel. The ministry of Rodney Griffin's song about God's faithfulness was his greatest help, just what he needed in his dark hour. He later would tell his pastor, "That's what pulled me through."

Have you ever wondered, when you hear moving Christian music, when this all began for the songwriter?

In the first and second grades Rodney took piano lessons but wasn't very motivated to practice. It became an ordeal for him – and for his mother. One day his mom tried to get him onto the piano bench for practice, but he was giving her all the reasons he didn't need to.

She finally said, "I want you in there practicing right now, and don't say another word." Eight-year-old Rodney, looked his mother in the eyes, put his hands on his hips, and testily said, "Word." He soon regretted that!

In the seventh grade, Rodney had a teacher who encouraged him to get back to his music. So he took piano again and seemed to get more out of it. This was for only a short school year, but it was enough to give him the understanding and background that would serve him well in his songwriting.

Then in high school as the president of the Fellowship of Christian Athletes organization on campus, he organized a choir and sang in his first quartet. His friends could see his love for music, and his enthusiasm and leadership kept his group strong. This was his first real taste of music ministry, and he loved it. He was hooked. Or maybe "called" would be a better word.

After Rodney's graduation with a degree in biology from Berea College in Kentucky, he worked for some time at Newport News Shipbuilding in quality control. This is where he wrote his first song. It may never have been one of the favorites, but it was enough to launch him on his adventure as a songwriter.

His first song was "When Will We Care?"

When Will We Care?

"How many times have you listened to a gospel hymn

And it led you to share Jesus with your lost friend?

But you failed to do this deed that your God commands

You didn't care about the little lost sheep in the cold, dark lands.

Chorus:

"When will we care enough to lead the lost sheep home?

We're the flock of God, and they're out all alone.

We are keeping something to ourselves, but it's not ours to keep.

When will we care enough to lead in his lost sheep?

"Now there's a sickness going 'round and it's called sin.

The basic symptom that you feel is no peace within.

But the medicine is Jesus Christ, at your heart's door he pecks,

Open up the door, receive His cure and you will feel no side effects."

(Words and Music by Rodney Griffin)

Of this song, written in 1989, Rodney says, "If you're a beginning songwriter, this should encourage you!" But Rodney kept writing songs until before long he was writing very good music, which God was using to challenge and melt and inspire hearts everywhere. Rodney's good friend Bill Gaither commented on Rodney's music. "I've heard it said that a generation is defined by its artists, and I believe that. We cannot overestimate the impact that artistic expression has on our world, which is why it is particularly thrilling for me to see a new generation of artists step up to their calling as Rodney Griffin has done. Rodney is a gifted young writer, and I am excited about the passion and perspective he offers through songs that bring us a greater understanding of eternal things. What he is doing is important."

Those of us who have been blessed by his music would agree!

"*After [Paul and Silas] had been beaten,
the magistrates ordered them thrown
into prison and told the warden to
watch them carefully until morning. …
The warden … ordered the guards to take Paul
and Silas to the maximum security block and
put them in a painful position by fastening
their feet in stocks.
That night Paul and Silas praised the
Lord that they had been found worthy
to suffer for Him because of the gospel.
They prayed and sang and shared the good news
of salvation with the rest of the prisoners.*"

(Acts 16:23, 25, *The Clear Word*)

CHAPTER 4

God Wants to Hear You Sing – 2

Watch for the new thing I am going to do.
It's already beginning to happen. Can't you see it?

(ISAIAH 43:19A *The Clear Word*)

DAVID RING, THE POWERFUL AND MUCH-LOVED SINGING EVANGELIST, has taught the world much about the impact of music. His life is the epitome of the value of praise and worship in the midst of adversity. Despite problems that could have destroyed him, Ring's ministry has impacted millions. Lives have been changed because of his faith.

You see, David has cerebral palsy. Many may see this as a debilitating neurological condition—and severely limiting. Even so, he receives 700-800 invitations each year to speak and to share his testimony, and to *sing!*

If you're not acquainted with this remarkable man, let me introduce you. David is the youngest of eight children, and because of his cerebral palsy, *everything* he does is done with great difficulty. Activities that anyone else may take for granted for David take enormous energy. Just speaking requires great effort.

His father, a pastor, died when David was 11. His mother was the mainstay in his life, and from her he drew the courage to go on, even though he often found himself the brunt of cruel taunts, jokes, and pranks of his thoughtless classmates. He knew he could always find refuge in his mother's arms and he always felt better after sharing his problems with her. She listened. She told him that God had a plan and purpose for his life, just the way he was.

But when he was 14, his mother died of cancer. Now his cheering section was gone, and he found himself with no one to encourage and understand him. He lived with a sister and her husband, and he often told them, "Just give up on me. I'm a no-good cripple." And David gave up on himself.

His sister told him, "David, I'm *not* giving up on you. I don't know what I'm going to do with you, but I won't give up." He had stopped going to church, and had become a truant, often skipping school because it was so traumatic for him to take the bus and then to stand up against the treatment he was sure to get on the playground and in the classroom.

His sister often invited David to church with them, and he always refused. But he says, "Just to get her off my back, I decided to go with them one Sunday night. I sat in the very back, and part of the time, I had my fingers in my ears. I remember hearing the preacher going on and on, and thinking, *I wish he would SHUT UP!*"

Yet despite the apparent coldness of his heart, the Holy Spirit was somehow breaking through. David found himself at the end of one evening service standing and making his way to the front for prayer. He says that that night in April 1970 changed everything, when the God of the universe kept His word to come into his heart and change his life completely.

Whereas before David had felt isolated and friendless, he now discovered that he had a sense of humor that drew other students to him. Everything was different. When he graduated from high school, he was vice president of his class and voted the most popular kid in school.

He admits, "Before my mama died, I depended on her for everything, but when she was gone, I discovered that God was more than enough for me." Before his conversion David was belligerent, shaking his fist at God and demanding to know why He had taken his mama, but now he understood that even through the pain and desperation, God was still there. And he discovered that God can do anything.

One night, when David was seventeen, he felt God's call for him to preach. He said, "I was lying in my bed, when I was sure God was speaking to my heart. He said, 'David, I want you to become a minister—an evangelist!'" David thought it was incredible that God would ask this of him. So this was his conversation with God, "Lord, I have cerebral palsy!"

And he thought God responded, "Oh, really? Tell me something I don't know, Buddy!"

The urging would not go away, and David began to believe that God had a specific role all mapped out for him. But it wasn't easy when he shared the idea with family and friends. His brothers and sisters told him to forget about it. They reminded him that he couldn't even pronounce the name Jesus clearly. But David didn't give up.

His professors at college didn't see much hope either. They tried to steer him into other careers, but David held on, took all the necessary courses, and completed his work. He says, "I squeezed a four-year college program into five." An amazing accomplishment for anyone in his shoes, because *everything* took monumental effort!

After graduation, David started telling his story in churches, and people were blessed.

One night a beautiful girl attended his meeting. She was a college student and had dated the football players on campus, but she was looking for some direction from the Lord for her life. She was impressed that David had something very genuine from God and wanted to get better acquainted with him. She met him at the table in the foyer as he was selling his tapes and other materials. Finding it very difficult to have a word alone with him, and trying without much success to break through the armor of protection he had erected, she finally asked him if he would like to have a soft drink with her at a place nearby. They soon found they had much in common, and Karen fell hard for this astonishing man whom God had brought into her life.

David's family had often told him, "You'll never get married. No one will want you." So it was hard for David to see himself as a happily married man with a family, but that is exactly what he is today.

God has done amazing things in the lives of David and Karen Ring. They have four wonderful children and are involved in an enormous ministry that only eternity can measure. David's whole life is based on the truth that when God says, "My grace is sufficient for you," He means it and is willing and able to take the most hopeless situation and change it into something glorious. David tells people everywhere, "Don't whine; *shine!*" There's power in praise, and there's power in a song. David's life is a testimony to the fact that in every circumstance God wants to hear us sing.

David has a wonderful way of describing the prison scene in Philippi found in Acts 16.

He says, "Paul and Silas were in the dungeon. They had been beaten severely, and placed in the stocks.

"Even in this miserable position, and with their backs bleeding, Paul turns and says, 'Silas, have you still got a song left in ya?'

"'Yup, I think I do,' Silas answers. 'What do you want to sing?'

"'Well, I don't know, but you start something, and I'll sing along with you.' So Paul and Silas started singing at midnight. It wasn't a wimpy prayer, whining and complaining to God because of what had happened. No, they were singing praises to God because He had trusted them with suffering. Their singing was so loud and clear that all the prisoners couldn't help but hear what was going on."

And David Ring says, "What's more, that song not only filled that whole prison, but it went out into the night sky. It passed the moon, passed the stars, and made its way all the way to heaven—right to the ears of God. And God was listening. He said to the angels, '*Shh, shh*, I think I hear singin'!'

"'Of course You hear singin', God,' an angel replied. 'We sing all the time up here.'

"'No, I hear singin' from a jail in Philippi, and I *like it*!' And God started tapping His foot!

"Now," David says with a big smile, "you're saying, 'Preacher, that is *not* in the Bible!' Oh yeah? The Bible says there was a great earthquake! What do you think caused that? God was tapping His foot to their singin'!"

David continues, "What do you do when the bottom falls out of everything? What do you do when you're faced with failure or loss or pain? You *sing*! God likes it. If we would thank Him more and praise Him, even in difficulties, it would make our faith stronger, and we would find that He will bless us even more."

Rodney Griffin wrote a song based on this powerful passage of Scripture.

God Wants to Hear You Sing

"The chains were fastened tight, down at the jail that night,

Still Paul and Silas would not be dismayed.

They said, 'It's time to lift our voice, sing praises to the Lord,

Let's prove that we can trust Him, come what may.'

"God wants to hear you sing, when the waves are crashing 'round you,

When the fiery darts surround you, when despair is all you see.

God wants to hear your voice, when the wisest man has spoken,

and says, 'Your circumstance is hopeless as can be.'

That's when God wants to hear you sing.

"He loves to hear our praise on our cheerful days,

When the pleasant times outweigh the bad, by far.

But when suffering comes along, and we still sing Him songs,

That is when we bless the Father's heart.

"God wants to hear you sing, when the waves are crashing 'round you,

When the fiery darts surround you, when despair is all you see.

God wants to hear your voice, when the wisest man has spoken, and says,

'Your circumstance is as hopeless as can be.'

That's when God wants to hear you sing."

(Words and Music by Rodney Griffin)

There was a time in David Ring's life when God showed him unmistakably that there is power in a song. He was driving to a small church one evening where he would speak. On the way, he stopped at the college where his girlfriend, Karen, was a student, and took her with him to the service.

On the way, he turned to her and said, "Babe, tonight I want to do something to bless the people. This is an itsy bitsy church in a dinky little town, and maybe they won't know the difference. Tonight, I'm going to *sing*!"

Karen was shocked because she knew that David couldn't sing, he was tone deaf and couldn't even carry a tune! But David was sure this was what God wanted him to do that night. So after he had given his message, he told the people that he wanted to sing for them. He asked the accompanist to give him an introduction. She asked what key he preferred, but he responded, "Just play it in any key, because before I get done, I'm going to be all over that piano." And David Ring sang publicly for the first time these familiar and powerful words:

> "I've heard an old, old story, how a Savior came from glory,
>
> How He gave His life on Calvary to save a wretch like me;
>
> I heard about His groaning, of His precious blood's atoning,
>
> Then I repented of my sins and won the victory.
>
> "O victory in Jesus, my Savior forever!
>
> He sought me and bought me with His redeeming blood;
>
> He loved me ere I knew Him, and all my love is due Him—
>
> He plunged me to victory beneath the cleansing flood."

David could sense that God was working. He just knew that God was saying, "Keep singin', Boy, I like it."

So David said to that small congregation of about 90 people, "Here's my favorite stanza:

"I heard about His healing, of His cleansing power revealing,

How He made the lame to walk again and caused the blind to see;

And then I cried, 'Dear Jesus, come and heal my broken spirit,'

And somehow Jesus came and brought to me the victory.

"O victory in Jesus, my Savior forever!

He sought me and bought me with His redeeming blood;

He loved me ere I knew Him, and all my love is due Him—

He plunged me to victory beneath the cleansing flood."

As David finished his song, there were many people standing and kneeling down front. He hadn't invited them to come for prayer, but they were spontaneously responding to the call of God as they heard David sing. He knew God liked it. Big men, with tears streaming down their faces, told him that they had told God that night: "Lord, You're using David Ring; please use me!"

David says to his audiences, "I have cerebral palsy. What's your excuse?"

The little churches which invited him to speak became huge churches, but still David was faithful to sing his song, even if there were hundreds of beautiful voices in the choir. And God has honored his message of faith and his song of victory in Jesus.

God wants to hear you sing. Praise changes *us*. Praise is the antidote for pride. David said in Psalm 90:14: "Fill us early in the morning hours with your love so we can sing your praise throughout the day and be glad the rest of our lives" (*The Clear Word*).

"Are any of you suffering misfortune? Take it to the Lord in prayer. He'll give you the strength to get through it." (James 5:13, *The Clear Word*).

Singing is prominent all through Scripture. King David and his army sang their song of victory *before* the battle. Psalm 20 is that song. "Sing to the Lord, all the earth; daily proclaim His message of salvation." (1 Chronicles 16:23, *The Clear Word*)

Praise changes our focus from ourselves and the transcient things of this world to the unseen but infinitely more real things of eternity. That's why God wants to hear you sing!

"Then Jesus ... said to the woman who

was still trembling in fear ...

"Where are all of those who were accusing you?

... There's no one here to condemn you."

She looked around and said, "You're right, Lord. There's not a one."

Jesus responded ...

"Neither am I going to condemn you.

You're forgiven."

(JOHN 8:10, 11, *The Clear Word*)

CHAPTER 5

Merciful to Me

"… I am the Eternal One … full of mercy and compassion. …
I am gracious and kind, not easily angered, overflowing
with love and forgiveness."

(Exodus 34:6, *The Clear Word*)

RODNEY GRIFFIN TELLS ABOUT A TIME WHEN HE WAS CAUGHT—
"red-handed, no alibi, and witnesses-present caught!"

When he was a kid, Rodney loved to visit his grandparents' home in the tiny town of
Eubank, Kentucky, especially when his cousins were visiting there also. A favorite way to
get some ice cream money was to find glass soda bottles along the roadside. They could get
10 cents for each soda bottle they returned to the country store, and that's how they bought
their ice cream.

But one day they found only enough bottles for one ice cream cone, and they needed a creative way to make some more money. That's when his older cousin spoke up, "Hey, I've got it! Grandma has a whole bunch of soda bottles in her pantry. She'd never miss them if we cashed them in. After all, she loves to watch us eat ice cream." So the plot was created.

Rodney explains, "Since I was the smallest, I was elected to sneak into Grandma's pantry and steal her bottles. My little heart was pounding all the way to the country store, but I could just taste that delicious ice cream, so I didn't care.

"But the problem with sin is that there is always a price to pay. When we got back to Grandma's house, we found her standing in her pantry, hands on her hips. She asked, 'Where are all my bottles?'"

The woman who was dragged to Jesus may have thought she could get away with her escapade. However, she and her nameless coward consort were spotted, and she was the one shoved out into the street for judgment. Her heart must have been pounding, her palms sweating, and her world spinning. But Jesus did the unexpected. He put it all to rest. He was merciful. She didn't get what she deserved; she got the gift of eternal life.

Rodney says, "I'm so glad Jesus has mercy, even when grandmas don't." In the Greater Vision song, "Merciful to Me," Rodney takes us back to this scene in Christ's life.

Merciful to Me

"The angry men were closing in, rocks were in their hands,
A decent payment for her sin—now her life must end.
But Jesus said, 'Let he who is innocent cast your stone today,'
I wasn't there to see her face, but I can almost hear her say:

"Merciful to me—when I deserved to die,
Merciful to me, my soul He brought to life;
Nothing could I bring, my debt to satisfy,
Jesus was merciful, merciful to me.

"Satan's men were closing in, I knew what was in store,
A decent payment for my sin, eternal fire, and more.
But Jesus said, 'I have an announcement, I'd like to make today;
I even have the scars to prove that I've taken this one's place.'

"Merciful to me—when I deserved to die,
Merciful to me, my soul He brought to life.
Nothing could I bring, my debt to satisfy,
Jesus was merciful, merciful to me."

(Words and Music by Rodney Griffin)

Linda and Tim were in their 30s and had good jobs and good health. They were in love, and looked forward to a bright future together. Tim was employed by a multinational corporation, and he spoke three languages. He was an outgoing, good-looking young man, and he soon found that he was quickly gaining prestige and respect within his company. It wasn't long, though, before he began spending more and more time away from home, and he became completely engrossed in his work. It was, after all, a heady trip.

Subtly he became a different person at home—exacting and critical. He was critical of their pastor and friends at church. His disposition began to change from kind and attentive to harsh and unloving.

Linda began attending church alone. Tim, if he was home, was too tired. Their home became a place of contention and unrest. Finally, Tim admitted that he was involved in an affair with his secretary.

Tim was unreachable. Unwilling to go with his wife for marriage counseling, he moved out, blaming Linda for the breakup and leaving her asking, "What could I have done differently to prevent his confusion and bad decisions? What can I do now for him, for myself, to heal the wounds that have been made?" Linda kept asking herself.

Linda didn't hear from Tim, or even about him, for nearly two years. Then she learned that he was in deep trouble with his employer. Because some of his decisions had caused the corporation to lose large sums of money, he was terminated. He left town, and Linda lost track of him altogether.

Tim's reputation followed him and it became impossible for him to get similar employment. As he sank into depression, he began trying to drown his problems with alcohol. Linda learned through a mutual friend that he was drinking heavily.

He tried his hand at the gambling in the casinos, and even had some luck for a short time, but then he started taking drugs. This brought him to an all-time low. Tim lost everything he owned while attempting to satisfy his craving for one more fix.

Tim thought of suicide but discovered he didn't have the courage to actually do it. It came as a shock to find that, on top of everything else, he was a coward.

About this same time, Linda was finding a new faith in God and a prayer partner in Roger Morneau and his wife. This author and man of prayer had long been an encouragement to her. They began praying together for her husband, whom she hoped was still alive. They prayed for Tim daily, asking for God's intervention in his life, for the forgiveness of his sins, and for his conversion.

Another year went by. Then one evening Linda, in her kitchen, was watching a national news program when the reporter interviewed a group of homeless people in a distant city. The people were living behind an abandoned factory near a highway overpass. The state was planning to demolish their shacks and move them elsewhere.

As she was cooking, Linda heard a familiar voice. Turning around, she was stunned to see Tim on the screen. If he hadn't spoken, she would never have recognized him. He wore a beard and had long stringy hair. He was filthy and looked like a tramp. Linda could hardly believe that the pitiful man she was seeing was the man she loved.

The interviewer asked how he was managing, and he said that he got most of his food from the garbage cans and dumpsters behind restaurants and stores. Linda burst into tears. It broke her heart to see him so thin and miserable, but she was thankful to learn that Tim was alive.

Linda intensified her prayers for Tim, asking God to open his heart. The next day she contacted the TV station and learned where the interview had taken place. Arranging to have some time off from work, she began to search for her husband. As she drove her car to the designated place, Linda found shacks, old broken-down machinery, and finally came upon a group of men warming themselves by a fire in a rusty old steel barrel. Was she safe here? With a prayer for protection, she locked her car and approached the circle of derelicts. She asked if they knew a man named Tim. One of the men pointed to a doorless shack not far away. Inside, after her eyes became accustomed to the darkness, Linda found her husband in a small, cluttered room, lying on a pile of broken-down cardboard boxes that he used for a bed. It provided at least some insulation from the cold of the pavement.

Tim struggled to sit up as Linda entered. Soon it began to dawn on his beclouded mind that this was his wife, the woman he had treated so shamefully. Linda knelt beside him and threw her arms around his neck. She said, "Tim, I love you. I will never let you go."

Telling of it later, Tim would say, "At that moment I understood the miracle of God's mercy and forgiveness as I never had before."

Stunned, Tim couldn't believe that Linda was really there and seeing him in this filthy place. He kept saying, "I'm disgustingly filthy."

It was late autumn in that huge eastern city, and a light snow was falling. The room was cold, and Linda begged Tim to sit with her in her warm car. He walked to the car, but only stood beside it; he felt too dirty to get in. Linda said he soon looked like a snowman.

"Will you sit in the car if I cover the seat with a blanket?" she asked. When he promised he would, she drove away and returned later with a warm blanket and hot food from a fast-food restaurant. The sight of him feasting on what he considered food fit for a king brought her both pity and joy.

Returning to her motel, Linda prayed harder than ever. Before retiring for the night, she opened her Bible again for something special. Glancing at some texts she had underlined, she found these words in Romans 8:11: "… He who raised Christ from the dead will also raise you from the dead through the same Holy Spirit, who's already in you." (*The Clear Word*)

That's it! Linda said to herself. Tim's mind needs to be re-created by the power of God's Spirit to what it once was—to the sound mind he once had. She knelt beside her bed. She was speaking with God in more and more specific terms.

Five days passed, and everything seemed at a standstill. Tim was too ashamed to go anywhere with her. Finally, she had an idea, and took a copy of Roger Morneau's book *Incredible Answers to Prayer* and read bits of it to Tim—stories of God's love and forgiveness.

Linda's prayers were being answered … dramatically. She asked God to bring healing to Tim, to take away his craving for drugs and liquor and to give him a sound mind. Tall order, but she knew she had a big God. Then she asked Him to bring Tim back home. It took a week before Tim agreed.

She said, "I couldn't stop the tears from flowing, as I listened to him talk and realized that the Holy Spirit was bringing my husband back from the dead."

She took Tim to a barber shop. She got new clothes for him, and he showered and began to look like a normal person once again.

She was able to get a transfer in her company, even a promotion, so they moved to a new location and began their new life together. Tim knew that only God's love through a willing and loving child of His could accomplish what he was seeing in his wife. It was the beginning of an era of marriage more joyous than either of them had ever known.

Unconditional love isn't easy. Only Jesus can bring someone to portray the magnitude of what mercy and grace look like. Anyone looking on could see not only how much Linda loved Tim but also could see the dimensions of the Father's mercy. A miracle indeed, and totally beyond our reach as weak humans, but because of His mercy "all things are still possible."

Tim experienced mercy and a strength that enabled him to build his life again.

He knew these words were true for him, as they are for each of us:

"Merciful to me—when I deserved to die,

Merciful to me, my soul He brought to life.

Nothing could I bring, my debt to satisfy;

Jesus was merciful, merciful to me."

(Words and Music by Rodney Griffin)

Adapted from *More Incredible Answers To Prayer,* by Roger Morneau. Review & Herald Publishing Association. Used with permission.

"Jesus answered,
'If you knew who was asking you for a drink
of water, you would be asking Him for a
drink of living water.' "

(JOHN 4:10, *The Clear Word*)

CHAPTER 6

He's Still Waiting By the Well

"The water that I can give you is special. Once you drink it,
you'll never be thirsty again."
(JOHN 4:14, *The Clear Word*)

TOMMY STEWART WAS EXCITED! He and his friends had been invited to lead a weekly prayer meeting in Paradise, California. Even though he was only 16 and his friends were all teenagers, they eagerly wanted to share something with the adults in this large church—something that had become meaningful to them.

They divided the group into small and random segments and then gave the group members a few minutes to get acquainted and comfortable in their setting. Each small group chose a leader and spent a little time praying together. Then each cluster was given a short passage of Scripture to study as a group. They began by reading the text and then set out to dig deeper. They asked questions like, What? When? How? Who? Where? Why? They allowed their imaginations to grasp the reality of the incident in Christ's life. They found the reality of the Scripture passage taking on new meaning. They affirmed one another as around the circle they each told of new insights on that particular biblical passage.

Then the teenager leaders asked them to pause for silent prayer. During this time they were to ask the Lord to speak to their hearts and give them a personal application to the story. Tommy urged them, during their silent prayer, to ask God "Who am I in this story? What personal lesson do You have for me from what I've discovered about Jesus?"

One of the favorite Scriptures that the teens and adults loved to study was the story of Jesus with the Samaritan woman at Jacob's well.

Rodney Griffin's song "He's Still Waiting By the Well" captures the emotion and the intimacy of this providential encounter.

"Jesus' feet were growing weary, as He journeyed on His way.
So He rested at a well side—a comfort in the heat of day.
There He waited for a woman, black with sin and bound for hell.
When she arrived, He plainly told her, 'What you need's not in the well.'

"He's still waiting by the well, and He's holding out His hand.
If you'll drink this living water, you won't have to thirst again.
He's been waiting by the well side—knowing you'd be passing by,
So take advantage of the moment—He's not gone, He's still waiting by the well.

"Are you tired of being thirsty, even though you've had your fill
Of the water that the world gives, does it leave you longing still?
Well, there's good news at the well side, a woman's voice rings loud and clear,
She says this man changed her forever, and if you need hope, you can find it here!

"He's still waiting by the well, and He's holding out His hand.
If you'll drink this living water, you won't have to thirst again.
He's been waiting by the well side—knowing you'd be passing by,
So take advantage of the moment—He's not gone, He's still waiting by the well.

(Words and Music by Rodney Griffin)

Shortly after all the groups got into the assigned Scripture passage, two women entered the foyer of the church. Realizing they were late and not wanting to disturb groups that were already working together, they turned to leave, promising each other that next week they'd get there on time. Tommy was in the sanctuary, praying for the groups. Looking up, he spotted the ladies just as they were turning to walk out. He quickly walked over to them and welcomed them to the Bible study time. They were a little embarrassed and explained to Tommy that they would come earlier the next week.

"Let's have another group—with just the three of us!" Tommy urged. "We can easily do it in the time that's left." So they went inside the church sanctuary, and the three of them had a great time together. As they were finishing, Tommy looked into their faces, smiled, and summarized some of the parts of the story that had stood out in their minds. But as he spoke he noticed that Mrs. Wallace's eyes were filling with tears, so he asked her how he could help.

"This is such a remarkable story, almost unbelievable, and it has touched my heart deeply," she responded. "I'm grateful for the way it has reached me, but I have a dear friend who is over in the Feather River Hospital right now, and I wish so much that she could understand this story. But she has never known Christ. She's dying of cancer, and now I'm afraid she'll never have an opportunity to know Him."

"Mrs. Wallace, *you* can share this with her," Tommy urged.

"No, Tommy. I know that you teenagers have been sharing the gospel with others, and I've been thrilled with the stories of what God is doing, but I've never led anyone to Christ, and I can't do this. You don't know my friend. She's always had a closed mind," was her adamant response.

"I'll go with you. I'll drive you over to the hospital, and on the way I'll teach this to you. If I can learn this, you can too. It's really not that hard." Tommy was convicted that he needed to help Mrs. Wallace fill her important role.

As they walked into the hospital, Mrs. Wallace again urged Tommy to do the talking for her. She said, "Tommy, you've had experience. You know how to do this. Please do it for me."

But she knew she didn't have a chance to back out. Tommy reminded her that Jesus' methods were always gentle. He was kind and compassionate. He got acquainted with people. He learned of their interests. He filled a need. He won their confidence, and then He said, "Follow Me."

"You are the one who has earned the right to do this. You are her friend. She trusts you, and she'll listen to you," Tommy reminded her. "I'm a total stranger. Why should she believe what I have to say?" Tommy was quite convincing. Mrs. Wallace knew that he had thought this through carefully. It wasn't that he was trying to avoid something *he* should do. Rather he was allowing her to do what only *she* could do.

"I'll tell you what," Tommy finally said. "I'll walk with you to her room, and then I'll find a chair and sit out in the corridor right outside the door. I'll pray for you while you're leading her to Christ." Tommy was obviously not going to budge.

It was settled, so silently Mrs. Wallace asked God to give her strength and to open her friend's heart. As she walked into the hospital room, it was a sad moment because both women knew they didn't have much more time to be together as friends. Mrs. Wallace lovingly told her friend about the evening Bible study and how much it had meant to her. She told the dying woman that God's free gift is still available, even though we will never be able to earn it or deserve it.

"Why should He want me now?" her friend asked. "I've never had time for Him, and now my life is nearly over. Why should I think that I can ask Him for anything *now*?"

By the way, that's a wonderful question, and we'll never be able to explain it. But the same Jesus who saved the Samaritan woman so many years ago is still "waiting at the well."

Mrs. Wallace shared a couple of Scriptures with her friend, praying that God would make the miracle of forgiveness clear to this needy heart. Then she asked, "Is there any reason why you wouldn't want to ask Him for this free gift that He makes available to anyone on planet earth—this gift of forgiveness and eternal life?"

Mrs. Wallace could see a new glimmer of understanding in the eyes of her friend. There were tears, too, of overwhelming gratitude. They prayed together as her friend repeated after her the sinner's prayer. What a moment! They both seemed to sense that this was much more than words shared in a hospital room in Paradise, California. This was a transaction with the God of heaven. And He is faithful who has promised.

As Mrs. Wallace and Tommy walked out of the hospital together a few minutes later, she was so overjoyed she could hardly speak. "This really works, Tommy. I wish I could have understood it and done this long ago. It really works!"

Tommy smiled. God had blessed them both that night with the gift of being used—of taking a friend by the hand—to the well, to find Someone who is still waiting there.

What an incredible thought! The same Jesus who was there for the woman of Samaria holds out the same hope to you and me. Every morning He says, "Come unto Me. Sit at My feet. I've been waiting for you, and I have a special message for you. I love you and I have a very special purpose for your life."

The next morning Mrs. Wallace's friend quietly passed away, but both Tommy and Mrs. Wallace had peace, knowing that she went to sleep secure in her newfound trust.

A question that many struggle with, including some Christians, is this: Can I really be sure that I am a child of God? Can I have the assurance of eternal life that some Christians seem to have? Ask Tommy Stewart. Ask the disciple John—his words are clear to us—recorded in 1 John 5:11-13: "But we believe what God said when He told us that He has given us eternal life through His Son. Anyone who believes in the Son of God has eternal life. … I wanted to point these truths out to you so you will know that as soon as you believed that Jesus Christ was the Son of God and accepted Him as your Lord and Savior, you were given eternal life." (*The Clear Word*)

This incident at the Feather River Hospital in Paradise, California, happened several years ago, and Tommy is now a medical student. His goal in life is to help others not only physically but also spiritually. Tommy knows Someone whose living water satisfies. He knows that there is Someone still waiting by the well, holding out His hand, and there is no joy like helping to place someone else's hand in His.

The story was adapted from *A Passion For Prayer*, by Tim Crobsy, Ruthie Jacobsen, and Lonnie Melashenko, Review & Herald Publishing Association. Used with permission.

"When I was in danger and put my trust in Him, He came to my rescue and helped me … Have faith in the Lord and be at ease. The Lord loves you and He is good."

(Psalm 116:6, 7, *The Clear Word*)

CHAPTER 7

God Wants to Hear You Sing – 3

*"When you go to your knees, God will help you to
stand up to anything."*

(Anonymous)

KURT FENTON AND HIS WIFE, LISA, from the other side of the world, share how the power of the message in Rodney's music touched their lives!

The Fentons are church planting missionaries from the United States but are now living in New Zealand with their three children. They had just returned to New Zealand in January 2004, after a six-month furlough in the U.S. Lisa discovered a lump in her breast, so on January 12, she contacted her physician for an examination. He confirmed her worst fears. No one wants to hear the word "cancer."

In February, after many tests, she was diagnosed with invasive ductile carcinoma. Lisa's surgeon ordered a lumpectomy as soon as possible. The team of physicians seemed to think that this minimally invasive procedure would be all that was necessary. But after the surgery, they made a new discovery—they were dealing with something even more serious—invasive lobular cancer.

The next strategy was for a double mastectomy, removal of both breasts, which the medical staff felt would be the only wise alternative in her situation. They told Lisa that because of her young age—38—she would be a good candidate for reconstructive surgery, which they would recommend.

Picture this: a little family, far from home, dealing with scary life-and-death issues, uncertainties, and a very real threat of death.

Lisa says, "During those first weeks after discovering the cancer, I went through all kinds of emotions. I found that listening to good Christian music and reading God's Word got me through. It took my focus away from my fears and reminded me that God is still on His throne and that His love for me is real.

"One of the songs that always brought tears to my eyes and became a huge challenge to me was 'God Wants to Hear You Sing.'"

"God wants to hear you sing,
when the waves are crashing 'round you,
When the fiery darts surround you,
When despair is all you see;

"God wants to hear your voice,
When the wisest man has spoken,

And says, 'Your circumstance is as hopeless as can be.'

That's when God wants to hear you sing."

(Words and Music by Rodney Griffin)

"I would listen to that song over and over and silently pray, 'Yes, Lord, I'm singing to You in the midst of my suffering.' I never really sang out loud—just in my mind—but the words and melodies were there."

In March they drove to Auckland, a five-hour trip, for the surgery. The surgeons felt that the procedure was successful, and Lisa began her seven-day recovery in the hospital. But on day two something happened, and she started to go rapidly downhill. She was extremely nauseous, weak, and couldn't eat. Each day was worse than the day before. She was given three units of blood at 1 A.M. on Saturday morning, but she felt even worse after that.

"I just wanted to die," Lisa would later say. "I was tired, sick, in pain, and ready to just go to heaven and be done with all of this. I somehow felt that God didn't love me anymore and had left me alone in my suffering." She was living in a world of gray clouds, but somehow managed to survive that whole day.

Kurt tells his side of the story: "Shortly after the long surgery, Lisa developed serious anemia, needing three units of blood. Then her right lung totally collapsed. This was a very low valley in her life—her strength to fight was gone. I thought I would lose her.

"She knew her complications were serious, and even though her physicians were working feverishly, she could feel herself slipping."

When Kurt left the hospital late on Saturday night, he really wondered if his wife would be alive the next morning. He was struggling with his own pain—the uncertainties and fears of losing the one dearest to him and the mother of his children. The next morning he went to church before he could get to see his wife. Later, when he walked into her room, her bed was empty. ... "Is she in the morgue?" He asked half out loud.

Here's what happened—the rest of the story, as Paul Harvey likes to say.

"After a difficult night," Lisa recalls, "I woke up Sunday morning just before 6 A.M. My husband would be at church, and I knew I wouldn't get to see him until after lunch. It was still a couple of hours before breakfast, but I didn't feel like eating anyway. I still felt pretty sick and the thought of facing another day like the day before was nearly more than I could bear.

"As I lay there in that lonely hospital room, the song "God Wants to Hear You Sing," started going through my mind, only this time the phrase 'God wants to hear your *voice*' struck me. I thought, *OK, God, You want to hear me sing? I'll sing!* (I'm afraid I didn't say it in the nicest way, either!)

"I started to sing my favorite hymn, 'Great Is Thy Faithfulness,' and I have to admit, it sounded pretty horrible. My voice was weak, my mouth was dry, my throat was scratchy. It was pretty squeaky at first, but I kept singing. I sang another song, then another, and another, and with each song my voice seemed stronger.

"By the time I had finished all the songs I could think of, I looked over to my window. The sun was just coming up and peeking through the curtains. There in the early morning quiet, I heard the birds beginning to sing. I felt that God's outdoor orchestra was just for me. He was singing back to me! Wow! I could feel His love and presence like never before. I was worshiping Him in my singing, and He was wrapping me in His arms of love. What a blessed moment!

"That morning I was able to get up, shower, and dress myself. I felt great! By the time my husband arrived at lunchtime, he couldn't find me. I was outside on the patio, sitting in the sunshine and reading my Bible. This was the first day I could read, because since the surgery I'd had trouble focusing. My eyes saw blurs, and I'd been in a fog with low hemoglobin and headaches. No wonder I wasn't thinking straight! My poor brain had been starved for oxygen!

"Physically I know I felt better because the blood transfusions were beginning to work, but more importantly I had improved emotionally and spiritually because God *does* want to hear His children sing. As the song says, 'When suffering comes along, and we still sing Him songs, this is when we bless the Father's heart!' I did, and I found that it really works. My spirit was lifted, and my whole world changed. God is so good!

"I have listened to that song almost every day since my battle with cancer began and every time it has been a powerful blessing to me."

Since Lisa's recovery, her prognosis remains good. She has been asked to be a support person, a counselor, for other cancer patients for the New Zealand Cancer Society.

She says, "I believe God will open many doors for me to share the gospel with other women who do not have the same hope that I have been so blessed to have. You can be sure I will share this song every time I have the opportunity."

Lisa holds tightly to the powerful words of Psalm 116:1-9:

"I love the Lord because he listens to me and hears my prayers.

He hears every time I call on Him, no matter where I am. So I will continue to call on Him as long as I live."

Sorrow surrounded me and pain engulfed me. I felt as if I were dying. Everywhere I looked I saw sorrow and trouble.

Then I called on the Lord and said, 'I beg You, O Lord, please save me!'

He heard me and saved me. The Lord is merciful and gracious; He is full of compassion.

The Lord protects those with childlike faith. When I was in danger and put my trust in Him, He came to my rescue and helped me.

So I will walk as in the presence of the Lord as long as I live."

(Psalm 116:1- 6, 9, *The Clear Word*)

"Jesus said, 'Don't be afraid. It was your touch of faith that made you whole. Go in peace and may the blessing of God be with you.' "

(LUKE 8:48, *The Clear Word*)

CHAPTER 8

Common Garments

"… The soldiers who had crucified Jesus took the few things He had worn and started dividing them up, but when they looked at His warm outside robe, they noticed that it was custom-made, seamless from top to bottom. So they said, 'This is too expensive a robe to tear and divide. Let's gamble for it.'"

(John 19: 23, 24, *The Clear Word*)

JEFF GRIFFIN WORKED IN THE NEWPORT NEWS Shipbuilding Company in Virginia as a QID inspector (quality control specialist). He married his beautiful sweetheart, Sue, and life seemed good—on the outside.

Jeff was an alcoholic, and it tinted everything in somber colors. At work, his life seemed carefree. He was pleasant, fun-loving, and always had a humorous story to tell. The problem was that they were usually off-color jokes. At home, things were not so funny.

Sue had become a Christian as a teenager, but as she saw her dreams of the ideal family dim, she came to the conclusion that this was to be her lot in life. She would do her best to be a good wife and the best mother she possibly could be for her two little ones, but she didn't see much sunshine in her future.

One day as Jeff was working in his office, a friend came in. Closing the door behind him, he told Jeff he had something important to say and wanted Jeff to listen. Quietly he informed him, "You know, Jeff, the boss likes you, but you're skating on thin ice. You're going to have to make some drastic changes in order to keep this job. The atmosphere around you is polluted with your bad language, and Bill has about decided to transfer you somewhere else—maybe out on the ships."

Jeff's first thought was, *"It's cold out there in the winter, and that's the last place I want to be!"* Jeff was puzzled. "What's wrong with what I'm doing?" He asked.

The answer was, "Jeff, Bill West is a Baptist deacon, and you often thoughtlessly use God's name in anger or in jest, and this is offensive to him. He believes in God and wants our place of work to be a positive, clean atmosphere. He doesn't like to see you living like this, Jeff. He doesn't like to see what you're doing to yourself and your family with your drinking."

"What in the world is a Baptist deacon?" Jeff wondered. That was a new one to him. But he was sure of one thing—he would *not* get transferred outside! And a plan began to emerge in his mind. *"How can I catch Bill at something?"* he thought to himself. *"I'm just sure he must be leading a double life. He can say these things, but how does he* really *feel? How does he* really *live when no one is looking?"* So Jeff decided he would watch, and watch he did. But to his dismay the harder he looked, the more aware he became that being a Christian was what made Bill different.

No matter what the problem, Bill would get his men together, motivate them, and send them back to their tasks. And Jeff could see that each of the guys was ready to do anything to please Bill. They liked him. They respected him. You could trust Bill to be there for you and to set an example of his expectations for his men. Wow!

Jeff was becoming confused. What made Bill West tick? He wanted to ask someone, but who? He didn't even have clear questions yet in his mind.

Then one day Bill asked Jeff, "Do you ever go to church?" Well, the truth was, yes, Jeff had been to church as a young boy, but he didn't have pleasant memories of that. Besides, God wasn't figuring very prominently in Jeff's life right at the moment.

"Jeff, why don't you come to our church next Sunday? Several of the guys you know from here are going to be there. They're going to give their testimonies."

"What on earth is a testimony?" Jeff wondered. But he didn't ask. He smiled and thanked the boss, but he couldn't get the idea out of his mind the rest of the day. What were these guys going to talk about?

"Honey, let's go to Bill's church on Sunday," Jeff said after work on Friday. Sue was shocked. The church was a 35-mile drive, quite a big deal with two small children, Rodney, 3 and Amy, 18 months. Sue was excited by this strange suggestion she was hearing from Jeff, but afraid to hope that anything would actually happen. Sue hadn't attended church for nearly five years and was eager to go. She wanted her children to know Jesus and to be surrounded with a Christian church family.

Throughout the years of their marriage, Sue had seen countless promises broken. Now she feared that this was nothing more than a passing fancy. But sure enough, when Sunday came, Jeff still wanted to go to church, so the four walked into the sanctuary and were ushered to a seat near the front. Jeff wanted to see these guys from work and find out what this was all about. Little did he know that he was an answer to their prayers. Bill had been asking God to bring Jeff and Sue to church, and here they were! Maybe this was miracle number one!

The Griffins were met with smiles, music, and God's Word. His fellow workers told their stories of how the God of the universe was actually their Friend! Their stories were different, but the same. Each told of a life changed and deep gratitude for the new direction. Jeff listened intently to every word. Could this work for him?

He decided to go back the next week, and each time he went something new seemed to click for him. The Holy Spirit opened his eyes and softened his heart just a little more each week, and Jeff began to understand and experience a little more of Jesus' love.

Years before, Jeff's mother had given him a Bible, and one evening he noticed it lying on the coffee table. Jeff wasn't sure just where to start, but he tried. "*If I go to the New Testament, I think that's the place I'll find the stories about Jesus,*" he thought. So he started with Matthew 1:1. It was hard work at first. Jeff was reading the King James Version, and he got a little bogged down in its centuries-old language. The first seventeen verses were difficult, but he read every word. Later, Jeff would say, "When a man is hungry, he'll eat just about anything." He was hungry, and he read on and on with deepening conviction. When he came to the words of Jesus in Matthew 11, the Lord seemed to say, "Jeff, this invitation is for you. Do you realize what I'm offering you?"

He read and re-read these words: "Come unto me, all *ye* that labor and are heavy laden, and I will give you rest. Take my yoke upon you, and learn of me; for I am meek and lowly in heart: and ye shall find rest unto your souls. For my yoke *is* easy, and my burden is light." (Matthew 11:28-30 KJV)

"My burden is light. My burden is *light*." This was a new idea to Jeff and really appealed to him. He was at last drinking at the "springs of living water," and he knew it. He was thirsty and dry, and God seemed to know exactly what he needed. A new birth took place in the living room that night. Jeff knew that something real had happened, a relationship was beginning with Almighty God! No one else could have known about the healing Jeff needed in his heart. Reading God's Word began the transformation.

Sue was watching, and daily she saw little changes—something new, something different. But always it was real. Her life was changing too. Now they had something for their children—a changed father and a new home life. Before, when Jeff had been drinking, he thought it was funny to give little Rodney a sip of beer. Sue could only watch helplessly, because when Jeff was drinking it wasn't a time for logic. But now all that was gone.

Jeff decided that God was calling him to leave the shipyard and become a pastor. A pastor? This hard-swearing, heavy-drinking shipyard worker, a pastor? But he did. He became a pastor—a good one—because he felt the calling of God on his life. Since 1974 he has been leading others to the same living water he found back when Bill lived the gospel, and then shared it with him.

Recently Jeff's church planned a special event for him to celebrate national Clergy Appreciation Day, and his church family presented Jeff and Sue with a very meaningful love gift. Then through a multi-media program, they showed the faces of many of the people in that church whose lives had been changed because of God's grace and because of the faithfulness of Pastor Jeff and Sue. It was an emotional moment as the people of that community poured their gratitude over their pastoral couple. As the faces of the many people were seen on the screen, Jeff and Sue's now grown son's song "Faces" was heard from a recent Greater Vision's CD.

Faces

"I dreamed my life was done, and I stood before God's Son,
It was time to see what my reward would be.
With love He reviewed my life, to count what was done for Christ,
For that was what would last eternally.

"See, I'd done my best to share that Jesus really cares,
And He would save if they would just believe.
Oh, but seldom did harvest come—so few did I see won,
Until the Lord said, 'Turn around and see.'

"Then He showed me the faces of the ones who'd come because of me,
So many faces that my life had led to Calvary.
All those years I thought nobody saw as I labored in lonely places,
That's when Jesus smiled and showed me all the faces.

"He said, 'Tho' you did not see the yield—you were faithful to plow the field.
At other times you helped Me plant the seed.
No matter how small the task, you did just as I asked,
And thanks to you these souls have been set free.

"Then He showed me the faces of the ones who'd come because of me,
So many faces that my life had led to Calvary.
All those years I thought nobody saw as I labored in lonely places,
That's when Jesus smiled and showed me all the faces."

(Words and Music by Rodney Griffin)

Rodney calls Bill West one of his heroes, because he is the man God used to lead his father to Christ. God still uses common everyday circumstances and common people to reach hearts with His good news.

Rodney says, "Some believe that if they're not especially gifted, God cannot use them! If you're one of those people, maybe my personal testimony will help. I was born into an alcoholic home. None of the talented Christians—preachers, singers, teachers—could reach my dad. However, (and I thank God for "however") God sent an everyday man, maybe like you, named Bill West, to work beside my dad at Newport News Shipbuilding, in Newport News, Virginia. Bill was a godly man. Though they were living two very different lifestyles, they developed a close friendship. So when Bill asked my dad to go to church with him one day, just out of respect for a friend and out of curiosity, my dad went. Soon my dad was forever changed by the power of God! And now for almost 30 years, dad has stood behind a pulpit each week, proclaiming that Jesus saves and has a plan for your life!"

As Rodney read again the story in Scripture of the woman who was healed just by touching Christ's robe, he thought about the garment. Just a common robe.

When he read the description of the crucifixion, he put himself into the scene at Golgotha. He heard the noise, the cursing, and felt the shame. As Christ hung in nakedness on the cross, the robe again is in the picture. The robe of Jesus made its way into the hands of a Roman soldier. As Rodney imagined this man walking off with that robe in his arms, it hit him! This is the same robe that the woman had touched and been healed. Yet there was nothing visibly special about the robe.

It wasn't the robe that had the power to heal. It was *who* was in the robe. Rodney Griffin bowed his head, and said, "Lord, would you make me a garment that You can live in and work out Your perfect will in me, from the inside out?" And then this song began to form in his mind. Of the hundreds of songs he has written, this is one of his favorites.

Common Garments

"One day a Roman soldier in a shameful gambling game
Won the blood-stained garment that once had clothed my King;
Just a cheap robe of linen, no great value did it hold,
But when worn by the Master, it was worth more than gold.

"You see, a few days before, this old garment had changed the life
Of a tired and helpless woman who'd believed with all her might;
She'd reached out and touched it with a hope to be restored,
She knew this plain old garment was the vesture of the Lord.

"God uses common garments to do uncommon things,
And God uses common people to live out His uncommon dreams.
It's not what you are now that matters, it's what He can make you to be,
For if God can take an old common garment and change a life,
Then surely He can use you and me.

"We are the reason that Jesus came to die,
And we have been chosen to send forth His light.
So it doesn't matter if your worth is great or small,
God needs some willing vessels, just common garments, that's all.

"God uses common garments, to do uncommon things.
And God uses common people, to live out his uncommon dreams.

It's not what you are now that matters, it's what He can make you to be,

Cause if God can take an old common garment and change a life,

Then surely He can use you and me."

(Words and Music by Rodney Griffin)

Rodney comments, "Did my family experience such drastic change because of an encounter with an outstanding, talented Christian? No! A common garment, named Bill West, simply lived a consistent Christian life in front of a nonbeliever, and that nonbeliever began to believe! I'm so glad God uses common garments to do uncommon things!"

"And God uses common people to live out <u>His</u> uncommon dreams!"

"Leave all your anxieties and worries with
Him because He cares for you."

(I Peter 5:7, *The Clear Word*)

CHAPTER 9

Let My Life Make a Difference

*"The God of mercy who invited you to share in
Christ's glory will equip and stabilize you firm
and steadfast."*

(1 PETER 5:10B, *The Clear Word*)

FROM HER LITTLE APARTMENT WINDOW, Janelle watched as the car pulled
away from the curb taking her parents to the airport and then back to Tennessee. As she
looked out the window at her neighborhood, at 5:30 in the morning, all she could see were
lights and shapes in her part of the huge city of Boston. She felt very small, insignificant,
alone, and just a little frightened.

"What now, God?" she asked, as she burst into tears. "This is my twenty-fourth birthday,
and I've never had to spend my birthday alone!"

She couldn't remember feeling so isolated from everything and everyone that was dear to her. Janelle sobbed as she thought about how long it would be before she would be with her family again. After washing her face, she looked into the mirror—the usually happy and very pretty eyes were not sparkling now. All her life she had dreamed of making a difference, accomplishing something significant for God. But how? On this bleak day, the chances seemed remote.

In exhaustion, Janelle finally slept, and as she slept, she dreamed. In her dream she sensed God's presence. He had a mission for her. He said, "Janelle, I want you to go out and buy a dozen of the most beautiful red roses you can find and then give them away—one at a time to people who need a special gift from Me today."

When Janelle awoke, the dream was still such a reality in her mind that she couldn't forget it. It seemed as though it could be a grand adventure, but with one major complication. The money she would need to purchase the roses was already designated—she had planned to buy some New Balance running shoes because she really needed them. She tried to argue with God, but it was useless. His plan was bigger. She knew it was something He was asking her to do *now*.

She finally found a dozen roses, hidden behind some other flowers at a grocery store. And they were gorgeous. Janelle's enthusiasm for this "project with God" grew as she paid for the roses, except that they cost the entire $50 she had been saving for shoes. But she was committed and now there was no looking back. As she left the store, Janelle seemed impressed that she should take the subway and look there for the faces of people who seemed to need God's special touch.

It was exhilarating to watch as she placed a rose in the hand of a tired little mother, then a homeless man. Each time Janelle would say, "This is a very special day for me, and I want you to have this rose." She wanted each one to somehow know that God was showing them His love.

One man, when given his rose, clutched it to his chest lovingly. Each person took the rose, some with tears of gratitude. Janelle was amazed to watch as God went with her to reach people whom He loved. In downtown Boston this was an amazing experience! Some were surprised but glad for the rose and the reminder of God's love. Janelle got off the subway and looked for people at the station or on the street who seemed to be God's "rose people."

With only one rose left, she found herself across the street from a large hospital. So she crossed the street and went inside. Walking down the corridor to the nearest nurses' station, she found a nurse there and asked, "Is there someone here I could see for just a moment? I have a rose I'd like to give to someone."

The nurse seemed very glad to see Janelle and walked with her down the hall. On the way, she spoke about a young man who, the physician had told them, would probably not live through the day. The patient's family hovered about the bed, speaking Spanish, a language Janelle didn't understand. She went to the bed, smiled, and placed the flower in his hands, with the same words she had already used eleven times that day.

There seemed to be a hush in the room, and Janelle knew that God had been leading her, not only throughout her exciting undertaking but also to this very place. To her surprise, tears ran from the young patient's eyes. In his weakness, he tried to hold and smell the rose, more grateful than she expected, and Janelle watched in awe.

As she left the room, the translator who had been in the room walked out with her and in utter disbelief asked her, "How did you happen to come here with the rose? How did you know about Carlos?"

Janelle had no recourse but to tell her the whole story. She told about the loneliness and devastation she'd felt when her parents had left. She mentioned the tears, the dream, and even the argument with God over whether to buy the shoes or the roses.

The translator's face paled as she heard Janelle's story. Smiling, the translator said, "I'm a part-time volunteer here. I come to translate for patients who cannot speak English. Today I asked Carlos if there was one last wish, one last thing anyone could do for him. He has a brain tumor, and everyone knew he was fighting a losing battle for his life.

"His only request was for a rose. No one seemed to know why. But in the busyness and all, I forgot about the rose." She cried with Janelle as they both realized the greatness of a God who loves us enough to send roses.

Then the translator added, "And Janelle, don't worry about the shoes. I'm a vice president of the New Balance Shoe Company here in Boston. You'll never need to buy any more New Balance shoes. Let that be my gift to you and to Carlos."

Janelle walked out of the hospital on a cloud. She had wondered what God was calling her to do with her life. She wanted a mission. She wanted to *know* that she was doing what He was leading her to do. As she got on the subway to return to her apartment, she silently spoke with God about what He had done for her that day. She prayed, "*Lord, this was such an amazing experience. I want to do this more. I want to reach people who are hurting, who need to have the sweet assurance of Your love. Are You asking me to be a hospital chaplain? I think I would rather do that than anything!*"

And so Janelle, through her own pain, learned that God would use her to reach others. Because of her loneliness, she could touch someone else who needed warmth, a friend, and a reminder of God's love.

Making a difference. Isn't that what life is really all about?

Janelle is now in training to be a hospital chaplain at Florida Hospital, and loving her work. Her life goal is still the message of Rodney Griffin's song:

Let My Life Make A Difference

"Let my life make a difference, let my love for Jesus shine.

Let the Holy Spirit mold me,

Let my life make a difference in someone else's life.

Let my life make a difference in someone else's life.

"I realize my life is like a Bible, and it's the only Bible some will ever read,

So help me, Lord, to live a life that's humble,

Only pointing them to Calvary.

Lord, I want so much to set the right example,

For I know their eyes are watching me.

Help me stay in the narrow way, my life a sacrifice will be.

"A certain man lay bleeding on the roadside.

He'd been beaten by some thieves who stole his clothes.

Two people walked on by who could have helped him,

But they chose the other side of the road.

Then a man passed by who made a difference,

A Samaritan who showed the heart of God.

He bound up his wounds and paid for his room,

Now there's a man who understands true love!

"Let my life make a difference, let my love for Jesus shine.

Let the Holy Spirit mold me,

Let my life make a difference in someone else's life.

Let my life make a difference in someone else's life."

(Words and music by Rodney Griffin)

It's amazing what God will do when we allow Him to be in control, to be truly *Lord*. He will take us where we never could have gone, to accomplish what we never could have done, and to *be* what we never could have been! What a mighty God!

"*O give thanks to the Lord.*
Lift up His name. Tell everyone
what he has done.
Sing praises to the Lord. Tell everyone the
wonderful things He has done."

(PSALM 105:1, 2. *The Clear Word*)

CHAPTER 10

God Wants to Hear You Sing—4

"God wants to hear you sing, when the waves are crashing 'round you."

(Rodney Griffin)

AFTER A CONCERT IN CALIFORNIA, Rodney got an e-mail message from Virginia Davidson, whose husband had died of complications from diabetes. He was only 47 years old.

Virginia says: "My husband was on life-support for the last week of his life. He had lived his life choosing to sing. And it is a choice—we can sing, or look at the circumstances and become consumed with the impossibilities. But he had chosen to sing, to look to God and to believe. His favorite song was "O, How I Love Jesus." So it was only fitting that as his life ended, it should be with singing.

"Our family and friends were gathered around his bed to say good-bye, and to give him our love and encouragement. And we encouraged each other as we sang. The angels seemed to be singing with us. There was a sweet presence of love in the room.

"My niece, who had no idea that it was his favorite song, suggested that we sing, "O, how I Love Jesus." She started singing, and I sang with her. Soon almost everyone in the room was singing. We sang one song after another until he slipped away. I know that God was with us in that room as we worshiped Him. He gave me such a sweet peace. My husband died almost three years ago, but that peace remains with me today."

She continues, "That's why the wonderful song, "God Wants To Hear You Sing" touched me so deeply. It took me back to that experience in the hospital room when we somehow *knew* He was with us, and He wanted to *hear* us sing."

Rodney says, "God wants to hear us sing, He wants to hear our praises and our worship. He wants to be the obvious center of our attention because He knows how much we need Him. We're His children, and the goal of this song is to help us picture our God with a great desire to hear from us, to hear our songs, our praises, our worship." The song says it well:

> "He loves to hear our praise on our cheerful days,
>
> When the pleasant times outweigh the bad by far.
>
> But when suffering comes along, and we still sing Him songs,
>
> That is when we *bless the Father's heart!*"

Our songs actually bless the Father's heart!

During a *PraiseFest* concert in Pigeon Forge, Tennessee, in November 2003, Gerald Wolfe read an e-mail message to the audience of 1,200, from a young sailor from San Diego,

California, who was on his way to Iraq. He and his wife were expecting their first child, and this seemed the worst possible time for him to be leaving home, and to be facing the uncertain situation ahead.

He and his wife said their tearful good-byes, and it nearly broke his heart. He struggled with his emotions as he watched the shoreline disappear in the distance. Finally he went below to his quarters and half-heartedly began unpacking his bags and getting his things organized. In his duffle bag he discovered something his wife had packed for him as a surprise. He was delighted to find a portable CD player and some Greater Vision CDs. He put a CD in, and stretched out on his bunk with his headset on. The words of the songs seemed to have taken on a new meaning. Each one seemed to be speaking directly to his heart.

When he got to the last track on the CD, "God Wants to Hear You Sing," he listened to it over and over, and was deeply moved by the power of that song. It seemed to have been written especially for him, for his lonely heart, for that specific day.

After listening again and again, he was able to really talk to the Lord in a way he hadn't done for a long time. He said, "Lord, You know how hard it is for me to leave home right now. You know all about everything, so I'm just going to give it all to You, and leave my wife, our child, my safety, my work, everything in Your capable hands. I'm going to trust You because You've promised in Scripture, that Your Word is true, and if we commit our plans to You, they'll succeed. I'm believing, and I'm trusting You to teach me to sing and to worship You, and to keep my eyes on You. I have nowhere else to turn. Help me to learn to sing to You right now."

In the days that followed, he found himself often singing with the Greater Vision trio, as he worked about the ship. Soon he noticed a very real change in his heart. God seemed to be telling him that this was a wonderful opportunity to serve his country with pride, to make a difference, to become a man of maturity and purpose, and to realize that God was still on His throne, still in complete control, and more than able to take his life in His hands. He saw a bigger picture— his opportunity to grow—spiritually, mentally, emotionally, socially, professionally, to mature, to accomplish something he could do in no other way. He vowed that with God's help he would rise to the occasion.

He e-mailed Gerald Wolfe, the leader of Greater Vision to tell his story, and to say "Thank You," to Rodney for the song. He said "Thank you for your ministry to me at a time in my life when I needed it so desperately. I'm going to hold on, and I'm going to sing!" This young sailor, whose name we don't know, was out on the ocean, with the waves literally "crashing 'round him." But he learned that God was there, and by looking to Him with a song in his heart, he was assured of his Father's presence.

Nearly everyone knows the name of Fanny Crosby, America's beloved, blind hymn-writer. But did you know that she wrote over 5,000 songs? She was a friend to presidents of the United States, but always took time to encourage anyone who needed her. Though she was blind, she chose to worship God through music. She suffered the loss of loved ones during the US cholera epidemic. When she lost her own year-old baby daughter to disease, still she sang, and she wrote her songs of worship. God gave her the "Blessed Assurance," that enabled her to write these immortal words: "This is my story, this is my song, praising my Savior, all the day long." No matter where you are, no matter what your needs or circumstances, God wants to hear *you* sing.

"God wants to hear your voice when the wisest man has spoken,

and says 'your circumstance is as hopeless as can be,'

that's when God wants to hear you sing."

Our God is the God of the impossible. He loves to take a seemingly hopeless situation, and change it, because He can do anything. He even told His people in Joshua 11:6 not to stockpile weapons of warfare, or horses for battle." He *wanted* His children to be at a disadvantage! They were to learn to look to Him for help. And when they did, He never failed them. He's the same today!

A struggling dad sent an e-mail to Rodney saying, "We just had a terrible storm that went through our area, but it was nothing compared to the storm going through our home right now. Our problem is with our oldest son, but God is showing me that even in the midst of our storm, He *does* want to hear us sing, and I thank you so much for this powerful reminder. I needed to hear that."

God's assurance in Psalm 132:11 is that He doesn't make promises carelessly or take them back. In Psalm 105:2, He tells us to sing praises to the Lord, and to tell others the wonderful things He has done.

> "Sing praises to the Lord. Tell everyone the wonderful things He has done."
> (The Clear Word)

That's why this story was shared by Dale McClung, a youth pastor in Independence, Missouri. He says, "My wife and I have three children—Amanda, 14, Josslyn, 10, and Bryson, 3. On December 11, 2001, we received the greatest challenge we've ever been handed. Josslyn was diagnosed with an inoperable brain tumor."

"The prognosis was not good. Untreated, the doctors offered her four to six months at best, and their best methods of treatment could only provide a twenty percent chance of her living for another one to three years. We were devastated, but God is good. He enabled us to never lose faith in His goodness. Somehow, no matter the pain, the uncertainty, the struggle, we have always believed that God was, is, and always will be—*good*! He somehow gave us the assurance that we were not alone in our struggles.

"About three months later, we got a Greater Vision CD—"Perfect Candidate," with the song, "God Wants To Hear You Sing," and this song touched me in a remarkable way. I have sung in a Southern Gospel group for five years, but I have never had a song take hold of me in this way. Our trio learned it, and we sang it for our church. Our church family knew all about our family's circumstances, and you can imagine the impact that the song had that morning. We have continued to sing it from time to time at the request of our pastor, and it always touches my own heart and bring tears in the congregation every time we sing it. This song has become a real strength in times of trouble, and an extra shoulder to lean on.

"I'm writing to you today to say THANK YOU for the dedication to write and sing the truth of the gospel of Christ, but also to offer great praise to God! We received news in September that there was a surgeon in New York who could perform a special surgical procedure on Josslyn's tumor. We traveled there on January 14 and returned on the 30th with a completely healthy and much-improved little girl! God is indeed good and wonderfully glorious, isn't He? Thanks so much for your continued hard work. It's making a difference."

Michele, who writes from Louisville, Kentucky, says, "This is my second year to attend the National Quartet Convention. I was blessed by your music there, and then later attended your concert in London, Kentucky. I knew I had to be there, and once again I left refreshed and with a renewed love for God. I bought four or five CDs that night because I knew I would need to listen to those songs again. That need recently surfaced, and your music is one of the things that is getting me through. We have experienced some turmoil and difficulties with relationships in our church with resulting anger and estrangements, but the one song that has helped me more than anything, is "God Wants To Hear You Sing."

I know that God is in control of this whole situation and He knows how it will resolve itself. We are His children, and He loves each one unconditionally. We want Him to be glorified in the solutions He provides. Until that happens, I am praising Him every day and trying to encourage my fellow church members.

"Music has always been a very important part of my life," Michele continues, "I've been singing in church since I was four years old, standing on a chair. Your music is an important part of our church fellowship. Thank you for your ministry and dedication. I am a testimony of how important your music and mission are."

Through *His* music, through heartfelt praise, God re-shapes our hearts and desires, and helps us to take on a strong family likeness —we actually belong to His family tree!

Psychologists tell us that when we spend as little as ten minutes with another person we become a little bit like that person. So, as sons and daughters of the King, our worship makes us more like Him, and helps us live like children of our Father!

"May the God of peace ...
equip you with everything you need
to do His will. May he help you to do
what is pleasing to Him through
Jesus Christ our Lord."

(HEBREWS 13:20, 21, *The Clear Word*)

CHAPTER 11

Survival Music

"I will never leave you nor forsake you."

(HEBREWS 13:5B, *The Clear Word*)

DO YOU REMEMBER THE STORIES ABOUT DAVID LIVINGSTONE, the great nineteenth-century missionary to Africa? We can't read his journal and not be inspired.

One night in the heart of that great continent, alone and in hostile territory, Livingstone could hear lions roaring and tribal warriors threatening. He wrote in his journal: "I have the word of a Gentleman, and I have peace. He has promised me, 'I will go with you wherever you go.'"

David Livingstone, as well as countless others of God's children, have experienced the truth that God *will carry us through* any difficulty, any need.

Many years after that great missionary and explorer took the gospel to the continent of Africa, another man and his wife, Joe and Patsy Budd, were asked to serve in Africa. Joe was to oversee the construction of churches, clinics, offices, and other buildings needed in areas where the growth of Christianity is explosive. Patsy was asked to work in a church administration office in the country of Tanzania.

Picture yourself 10,000 miles from home. You're in the heart of Africa, in a totally different culture. Joe and Patsy worked there for seventeen years and struggled to adjust to a completely different setting from their home in Wisconsin. It was challenging and rigorous work. Patsy's job kept her in Arusha, Tanzania, while Joe's construction sites were often great distances away. It was not unusual for them to be separated for months at a time.

Although the weather was oppressively hot and humid, Joe toiled doggedly through his days with his workers. His "home" on the job was usually one small non-air conditioned room with precious little ventilation. He seldom had even the luxury of an overhead fan. He would have given almost anything for a cool breeze on some nights. And it was lonely work. He was beginning to learn some words in these new tongues, but many of his workers were not Christians and didn't share his beliefs or values—or his language.

In his tiny, stuffy room, Joe read his Bible every morning and evening, and he *sang*. The words of the songs often seemed to be God's special communication with His tired, lonely, and faithful servant. Patsy was sometimes several days' journey away. It may have been only a few hundred miles, but in his little room, with only the sounds of the braying donkeys and the constant night noises, the distance seemed like a million miles.

One song written by Fanny Crosby in 1875 became a favorite of Joe's, and he sang it often because it brought him special comfort:

"All the way my Savior leads me;
What have I to ask beside?
Can I doubt His tender mercy,
Who through life has been my guide?
Heavenly peace, divinest comfort,
Here by faith in Him to dwell;
For I know whate'er befall me,
Jesus doeth all things well;
For I know whate'er befall me,
Jesus doeth all things well.

"All the way my Savior leads me;
Cheers each winding path I tread;
Gives me grace for every trial,
Feeds me with the living bread;
Though my weary steps may falter,
And my soul athirst may be,
Gushing from the Rock before me,
Lo, a spring of joy I see;
Gushing from the Rock before me,
Lo, a spring of joy I see.

"All the way my Savior leads me;
O the fullness of His love!
Perfect rest to me is promised
In my Father's house above;
When I wake to life immortal,
Wing my flight to realms of day,
This my song through endless ages,
Jesus led me all the way."

Somehow through the words of Scripture, his prayer time, and especially through the singing of these hymns of faith, Joe's energy was renewed each day. This became his morning and evening place of meeting with God, and he knew he was not alone. Singing to the Lord lifted him above his surroundings and developed into a daily routine he called his "survival music."

In Botswana he built an outpatient clinic, which consisted of a metal frame structure with block walls. It was built using the metric system, which was another adjustment for Joe. Usually all building materials had to come from South Africa, and the construction labor was done by the local people. His greatest stress came from trying to supervise all of the jobs being done at once—masonry, carpentry, plumbing, wiring, roofing, painting. It was all simultaneous and done by people who spoke a different language from his. How to be everywhere at once? And Joe needed to check constantly for accuracy.

Each morning before work as the workers arrived, Joe gathered them together in a circle for a short devotional time. Fortunately, he usually had a good translator. Joe would lead them in singing a sacred song, read a Bible verse, give an illustration of its meaning, and pray.

The translator chose the songs because he knew the ones that most of the crew could sing. There were no hymnbooks, but because generations earlier, when David Livingstone had been there and others since, many of the people had learned something about God. Many remembered some of the hymns of the Christian faith, though not a lot. Most of the workers loved to sing, and many sang well. Joe was often surprised by the rich harmonies these impromptu choirs produced.

One particular Friday morning was payday. This was always a bit of a hurdle because the workers were paid in cash and in their currency, which had to be calculated very carefully. Joe recalls, "That morning when I was feeling so discouraged, I was amazed to see how God came to my rescue. The men sang a song that then was new to me. It was written by Charles Wesley in 1741, but that morning I was sure that God had given Wesley that song just for me. I listened as the men and my translator sang these words:

> "Father, I stretch my hands to thee,
> No other help I know;
> If thou withdraw thyself from me,
> Ah! whither shall I go?"

Joe says, "Through this song, God provided divine help when my human resources were not equal to the task. He provided help for my time of emergency. And His divine assistance came through this song. As the men were singing, God impressed those words on my heart. I was saying with my men, 'Father, I stretch my hands to thee, no other help I know.' I am here for You, and I do believe that You are right here with me.

"By singing those words, and reminding myself and God that *I do believe*, something happened in my life that morning. God touched me in such a deep way that I knew He would meet my every need."

Joe continues, "I will never forget that very special morning when God did not withdraw Himself from me when I had nowhere else to go. Suddenly the clouds parted, and I knew He had given me renewed strength and encouragement. An interesting thing happened that day because God was speaking to the hearts of my men, too. Those who were not Christians had been learning these songs, hearing God's Word, and entering into the experience of prayer each day. Some of them gave their hearts to Christ. I could see changes in their behavior. One morning not long after that as we finished singing the song, 'When the Roll Is Called Up Yonder,' one man called out, 'When the roll is called up yonder, *I'll* be there!' He understood the message of the song, he gave the Lord his life and his wrong ways of living, and he began attending church faithfully. Others followed his example."

Joe will be looking for this Christian brother and others from Africa when the roll is called up yonder.

Joe had the sweet assurance that God would carry him through any need. He would make him strong in *His* strength. And He has carried him through. The message of Rodney's song has become a reality many times during difficult days for Joe and Patsy. The words apply to you and me, too.

You'll Carry Me Through

"Lord, when I first met You, I thought my troubles were over,

But I soon found that sorrow, heartache and trouble still lingered,

Though I was walking with You.

"I discovered what a comfort You were in those hard times,

And now my faith is tested and true.

So as I enter this valley, this old, familiar valley,

I've learned, Lord, just what You'll do.

"You'll carry me through, Lord—like You always do, Lord.
You'll hold me and hide me, like good shepherds do.
This valley's no different than all those valleys that came and went.
I know You'll be true, like You promised You'd do, You'll carry me through.

"How can I make it through the storms, without Your help, Lord?
From whom could I borrow the strength in my sorrow,
If my strength wasn't coming from You?

"So, Lord, I'll keep trusting, 'cause I know You'll be listening,
When this little lamb's calling You.

"And when danger is nearing, my cry You'll be hearing,
And I've learned, Lord, just what You'll do.
You'll carry me through, Lord, like You always do, Lord.

"You'll hold me and hide me, like good shepherds do.
This valley's no different, than all those valleys that came and went.
I know you'll be true, like You promised You'd do,
You'll carry me through."

(Words and Music by Rodney Griffin)

"... The people of God will sing,

"We praise you, Lord!

... We will trust You and not be afraid.

The Lord, the Lord God. ...

He is our song and our redemption."

(ISAIAH 12:1, 2, *The Clear Word*)

CHAPTER 12

Without A Valley

*"Don't worry so much about everything. When you pray,
ask God for what you need. Don't be afraid to plead
with Him, but always do so with a grateful heart.
God's peace … will guard your hearts and keep
your minds on Jesus Christ."*

(PHILIPPIANS 4:6, 7, *The Clear Word*)

TERI WEBSTER AND HER HUSBAND, TEDD, were living in Fort Lauderdale, Florida. After 10 years of marriage, they were excited about the pending birth of their first child. They had waited a long time for this day, and now in Teri's seventh month everything seemed to be going great. The nursery was ready, with each piece of furniture waiting to be called into duty. Teri, an occupational therapist, has a flare for decorating, and the nursery smiled in anticipation.

But early one morning in that seventh month, when everything seemed perfect, Teri was showering before going to the hospital where she worked. Suddenly she knew something was terribly wrong, and she crumpled to the floor in pain.

As she and Tedd rushed to the emergency room, through blinding tears she prayed and tried not to think of the worst—but she knew. The hemorrhaging clearly indicated that something was very wrong. The pregnancy was terminating too soon, and she discovered that her baby daughter was dead.

When the physicians confirmed it, Teri and Tedd were devastated. Their baby girl would never have a chance to live and grow up and be part of their family. Teri was forced to say goodbye before she ever had the chance to say hello.

Where do you go with this kind of grief? Teri turned to her God, and He gave her a song. Amazingly, in her darkest hours one special song kept coming to her mind, and she played the CD again and again until the words became part of her.

When her world seemed to be dark and lonely, without the warm bundle to hold in her arms, Teri would picture that little face smiling up at her. When she thought she couldn't go on because the pain of separation was so sharp, she would pray and then reach for the CD that she always kept close. Each time she heard the song it was like the promise of Jesus to her heart. He seemed to be saying, "Hold on, Teri, I know you're hurting, but someday an angel in white is going to come to you and put a darling baby into your arms. I know your arms are aching now to hold her, but hold on, I'm still with you, and I won't let go."

Teri drew new strength from the song and from the reality of heaven, where she would hold her baby daughter and they would enjoy the time together that they were not given here on this earth. The message of that song, "The Promised Land," by Larry Bryant and recorded by Terri Gibbs, brought true healing to her brokenness. The words painted a picture she could almost see. In his song about heaven, Larry Bryant gives a pristine panorama of green grass, and trees with endless shade, and crystal waters. Each verse ends with the positive declaration, "I'm going there!"

A year later, Teri had a dream so real that when she awoke the next morning she could recall every detail. It was such a happy dream she could hardly wait to tell Tedd. At breakfast she shared her exciting dream. She had seen Jesus standing in a beautiful place. He was smiling, and He called her name. When she approached Him, He gave her a baby wrapped in a pink blanket. He said, "I know you've lost someone special, but I have a new gift for you. 'This is Jessica Rae, and she belongs to you.'" With her joyful heart bursting, Teri recalled these happy moments and the reality of the dream. In her dream it seemed she could even "feel" the weight of the baby in her arms.

Jessica Rae, a beautiful little brunette, was born nearly a year later, on September 29, 1990, and she proved to be all that Jesus had promised. What a joy! And two years later their son, Jordan, was born. Two beautiful children!

Teri and Tedd look back on those dark days, realizing that they were a blessing in disguise. Through their valley, through the pain, they found a closer relationship with Someone who was always there for them.

Rodney Griffin's song "Without a Valley" describes their journey. Christians are not exempt from the pains or distresses of life. They experience heartache and frustration, too, but they also discover something deeper, something powerful, something even necessary to our growth and His glory.

Rodney says, "I always thought I wanted to sing. When I was a boy, I heard the

Cathedral Quartet and others, and I felt something stirring inside. I knew I wanted to be a gospel singer when I grew up.

"Years passed. Opportunities went by, but the desire to sing did not. I was sure that I was just not good enough and went to college and studied biology. I was sure I just wasn't cut out to be a singer. I was settling, but unsettled. Finally, when I thought time had run out, an opportunity came, and I saw this as God's open door for me.

"I started traveling … and learning. I learned what it's like to shower at a truck stop. I learned what it's like to sleep in a stranger's home. I learned what it's like to be stranded in a broken down bus along the side of the road. I learned what it's like not to see home … for weeks. I learned how to smile and sing when you have a headache. I learned to treat a handful of listeners as if they were a thousand. I learned what it's like to live in close quarters with other members of the group. I learned what it's like to be flexible. But through it all I learned something that is absolutely priceless to me. I learned that I *did* want to sing. You're not surprised? I was. You see, before I had been through the fire, I just *thought* I wanted to sing. At that point I had experienced none of the inconveniences that I now view as everyday life. Now I *know*, and it's a great feeling—assurance! So it goes with God.

"We say God will be with us in the rough times. We mean well, but if we've never had to leave the lush rose gardens of comfort, we just *think* we know that He'll be with us. However, ask the man who's been in the valley, and he can speak from a different perspective. He knows. He's heard God's voice of comfort. He's felt God's peace. He's held God's hand. He's ridden safely across. And that was the inspiration for this song. You see, God is so confident of Himself that He allows us to be put to the test. Why a test? Because He knows that the test will only prove that He is just as faithful as He said He would be. When it's all said and done, you won't just *think* He is faithful—you'll *know* He is."

And Teri and Tedd know, because of their valley.

Without a Valley

"I've been walking thru a valley,
It was dark and it was drear;
Yet in the middle of my sorrow,
I heard Jesus say, 'Child, I'm still here!'

"But without a valley, how would I ever know
That His strong and gentle hand will never let me go?
How would I know for sure that I'm secure
and safe where'er I go?
Without a valley, how would I know?

"So I thank You, Lord, for each trial,
How You're teaching me Your perfect love;
You have shown that I can still have joy inside
Even tho' the road seems long and rough.

"But without a valley, how would I ever know
That His strong and gentle hand will never let me go?
How would I know for sure that I'm secure
and safe where'er I go?
Without a valley, how would I know?"

(Words and Music by Rodney Griffin)

There is power in a song. There is power in praise. Maybe for you this old hymn holds the secret—in praise and in singing, we have Someone with us.

"In sorrow I wandered, my spirit oppressed,

But now I am happy—securely I rest;

From morning till evening glad carols I sing,

And this is the reason—*I walk with the King!*

"I walk with the King, hallelujah!

I walk with the King, praise His Name!

No longer I roam, my soul faces home,

I walk and I talk with the King."

> "[Jesus] called out in a loud voice,
> "Lazarus! Come out!"
> Then Lazarus appeared at the entrance of the cave,
> wrapped in his burial clothes."
>
> (JOHN 11:43, 44, *The Clear Word*)

CHAPTER 13

My Name Is Lazarus

*"Finally, be strong in the Lord and stand in
the power of His might."*

(Ephesians 6:10, *The Clear Word*)

ONE OF RODNEY GRIFFIN'S SONGS that almost instantly became a favorite is "My Name Is Lazarus." The song is a ballad of a familiar and powerful story in the life of Jesus and His friend, Lazarus. It finds Martha and Mary, Lazarus' sisters, in a heartrending situation as they grieve over the death of their brother. But the presence of Jesus changes everything.

Rodney worked on the song for weeks, and its melody and words inspire hope in those who hear it, just as the miracle did in Bethany when Christ spoke the words, "Lazarus, come out."

"My Name Is Lazarus" became the number one favorite on the charts of Southern Gospel music, and it remained there for weeks as Christians heard it in concerts and as radio stations played it again and again. Here are the words as you may remember them:

My Name is Lazarus

"One day four men brought a crippled man to Jesus.
Still and lifeless, he lay upon his bed.
He had not moved since he was just a baby,
Still he longed to become a normal man.

"Now we don't know much about the men that carried
The corners of his tattered bed that day,
But if we may create an illustration,
We'll see what these men might have had to say.

"Suppose that first man said, 'I hate to doubt it,
For Jesus touched my eyes when I was blind,
He made me see, and there's no doubt about it,
But this man's needs are more serious than mine.'

"Suppose that second man said, 'No need to bother;
This man's condition will remain the same.
Though Jesus touched my hand when it was withered,
I don't believe He can heal a man so lame.'

"Suppose that third man said, 'I hate to question,
But no one here is more skeptical than me;
Though Jesus cleansed me when I was a leper,
This helpless man will never walk, you see.'

"Then every eye was turned to the fourth man
To see how he might criticize and doubt;
But all three men were startled with amazement
When that fourth man stopped and said his name out loud.

"He said, 'My name is Lazarus; could I testify?
My name is Lazarus, it feels good to be alive!
When I in chains of death was bound,
This Man named, Jesus, called me out.

"If you think your little problem is too big for Him to solve,
Take it from the one who's heard the mighty voice of God.
I'm a living testimony of His death-defying touch,
My name is Lazarus!'"

It is common for audiences who hear the song to come to their feet in a standing ovation as the voices of Greater Vision swell with the final words of this powerful testimony of a man raised from the dead.

A young shepherd boy named David learned, too, that no problem was too big for the Lord to solve. Even though King Saul and his army were terrified when they faced a threatening giant named Goliath, David strode confidently out to face him. Face to face with this huge man who was bent on his destruction, he said, "You're coming to fight me with a sword, a spear and a javelin, but I'm coming to you in the name of the Lord, the mighty God of Israel, whom you've defied and cursed." (I Samuel 17:45, *The Clear Word*).

Right there on the battlefield David shouted his warning to Goliath and assured him the Lord would bring victory so great that the whole earth would know about the true God. He reminded the army of Israel that the battle was the Lord's. As the Israelite army cowered in fear, David *ran* to meet the Philistine giant. David knew he was not alone.

Charles Haugabrooks has a story. Charles was born twelfth in a family of 14 children. When he was only 3 years old his mother died in childbirth, and to fill the empty place in his young heart Charles began—at three—to sing. He's been singing all around the world ever since. As with all gospel singers whose music is their testimony, Charles loves to sing every time he gets the opportunity.

Charles had made a commitment to sing several times at a large convention of health-care professionals in Florida. Soon after making the appointment, a sister to whom he was especially close was diagnosed as having an aggressive form of cancer. As the days passed, her condition worsened, and Charles spent much time at her bedside, singing to her and talking about the wonderful future they would share together one day.

As the time approached for him to leave, he faced a dilemma. Her condition continued to deteriorate, and she grew weaker. Should he leave her side and risk having her die while he was gone? Should he stay with her and disappoint the hundreds who would be waiting to be blessed by his music?

It was a tough choice.

The day before he was to leave for the convention, she died.

In some ways the decision was now even more difficult. Could he go and bring inspiration to the audience while wrestling with his own deep grief? Could he be away from his family as they shared the loss during the funeral service of this beloved sister? Could he bring messages of hope to his listeners while his own heart struggled with this personal sorrow? Could his ministry be genuine and his smiles authentic? He decided that in God's strength, the answer to those questions was Yes.

In meeting after meeting Charles would stand before his audience and pour his hope into his songs. Though they knew nothing of his loss, they could somehow sense a special fervor in his music. "Oh, how I love Him, how I adore Him …" was a favorite both for him and for his listeners. He sang it several times throughout the week. Its powerful message seemed to have an anointed meaning as he sang.

At the final service, after his song, the platform manager stepped to the microphone and told the audience that Charles had come to the convention and ministered to them all through the week even while carrying this heavy personal load of grief. The audience knew they had been witness to a miracle. Here was a man whose walk with God was so genuine that he could trust Him—and still sing, even at midnight.

Charles Haugabrooks was "strong in the Lord, and in the power of His might." He is living proof that the promise of God is true: He does not leave us nor forsake us. Someone was giving Charles the peace to sing even when the way was dark. And someday Charles and Lazarus will no doubt have a very interesting conversation.

"[Jesus] stood up and removed His outer robe, took a towel, tucked it in at His waist and prepared to wash His disciples' feet. … He poured water into a basin and washed each man's feet and then dried them with the towel that was at His waist … He knew which one of His disciples would betray Him."

(John 13:4, 5, 11, *The Clear Word*)

CHAPTER 14

He Washed My Feet

"I will sing about the Lord's mercy and justice.
I will sing about you, O Lord."

(Psalm 101:1, *The Clear Word*)

THEIR MARRIAGE WAS ARRANGED. Without any knowledge or decision from the bride or groom, the royal family arranged for their prince to marry Princess Amelia in just a few months. Her country lay more than a thousand miles away at a time when travel was difficult and slow.

The prince's parents had done their work carefully and felt certain that she was perfect for him. As a privileged and beautiful daughter of royalty, they reasoned, Amelia's entire life had been a preparation for the role she was destined to play as part of the royal family in their land.

Her parents agreed. The day was set for the king's entourage to arrive and escort her on the long journey to her new life. Amelia dreaded their arrival, dreaded the moment when she had to say goodbye to the only life she knew. She was neither ready nor willing to leave her family to marry someone she had never seen, did not know, and certainly did *not* love.

Sensitive to the heart of a young woman, the king had done what he could to make her transition as smooth as possible, yet Amelia found it unbearable. Every hoof beat, every turn of the wagon's wheels took her away from the country she knew and loved … farther from *home*. That the king had commissioned a servant to be her personal escort and to take care of her every need made no difference to her. So heavy was her heart with depression and anger that she could hardly be civil to the man. He would anticipate her needs, but she would rebuff him with rude words and cold scorn.

Even though he was not appreciated, the servant took good care of his charge. When riding during the hot afternoons, he would place a canopy over her head to give her shade. He would bring clear, cool water to quench her thirst. When the rains would come, he would hold a covering over her to keep her dry. And every night he would prepare a comfortable place for her to sleep, arranging guards so that she could sleep without noise or fear.

Gradually Amelia noticed his kindness. During the long, slow hours of travel, she had time to think, and she grew amazed that he would befriend her even though she treated him so badly. At last Amelia opened up enough to ask him about it. He replied that as a servant of his majesty the king, it was his happy duty to do his best for the family. He said that he had served the royal family for some time and had always been treated fairly. "Now," he said, "I want to repay their kindness."

The days slipped into weeks, and every hour brought Amelia nearer to her new life. Despite herself, Amelia began to see beauty in the new lands they crossed and a friend in this kind servant who would always put her needs ahead of his own. She would watch him handle people and problems, seeing both courage and gentleness in his manner. Little by little she opened her heart to him and was surprised by the depth of his understanding of her hurts and frustrations. She grew to depend on him, and that made her feel strong. No matter her concerns, he would quietly listen, and he seemed to care about her and her feelings.

The more time they spent together, the deeper became her attachment to him. He was the only person Amelia could depend on in the strange new world she was about to enter. Her heart was touched as she poured out her life and thoughts to his listening ears. Gradually she came to find genuine love in her heart for this kind man who meant far more to her than a servant. He had become her friend, and more.

On the final night of the journey they camped within sight of the city. She could barely make out the shining palace he pointed out to her. He told her little anecdotes about the royal family. The next morning as they neared the palace she clung to the servant and whispered that she loved him. "Throughout these months of travel," she said as she wiped away tears, "you have been so kind and understanding. I love you. I can't endure the thought of being separated from you. If I had the right to choose, I would marry *you*."

He murmured words of comfort and courage, but she brushed them aside. "Compared to my feelings for you, royalty means *nothing*," she wept, "but I'm denied the choice to marry the one I love." They both wept as he tenderly kissed her goodbye.

Amelia was led to a beautifully furnished room. She bit her lip as she looked around, willing herself to be strong. Maidservants brought water for washing and fruits and bread for her to eat. She was urged to rest, for the festivities would begin in the morning and she would be presented to the king, the queen, and the prince whom she would marry. For a long time after they left she sat in darkness at the open window, looking down at the city that was now her home.

The next morning fresh flowers adorned the huge palace room, and everyone was dressed in their finest. An orchestra played in one corner, while the king and queen sat on carved chairs awaiting the arrival of the new princess.

Amelia had awakened before dawn with tears on her face from crying in her sleep. Only a lifetime of discipline made it possible for her to arise, wash her face and hands, and gently greet the servant who brought sour milk, breads, and raisins for her breakfast. Her eyes were still red when she finally allowed the ladies-in-waiting to dress her in a beautiful flowing gown and apply their expertise to her long hair. With subtle make-up and soft perfume, she felt a little better. A glittering tiara was placed on her head, and the picture was complete. Truly, she was a regal bride.

In the distance the music swelled, and Amelia let herself be led through hallways and down staircases onto the main floor. Her escort stopped at the doorway to a lavishly appointed room. He spoke briefly, going over protocol one last time. Now she must take her place beside the king and queen and await the dreaded moment when the prince would arrive.

Picking up one reluctant foot and then the other, she forced herself to walk through the doorway and down the wide aisle to the applause of the waiting crowd. She felt welcome, but also unwilling. The jeweled tiara pressed heavily on her head, but a lifetime of training enabled her to stand tall like the princess she was. At last Amelia reached the royal couple. She knelt, eyes to the floor. At the king's word, she carefully arose and turned to face the doorway.

A hush fell over the crowd. The orchestra paused for a heartbeat then began a triumphant march. Though she held herself like a princess, her eyes studied the mosaic floor. She could not, she would not, bring herself to look at the prince as he entered. The thunderous applause of happy subjects told her that he had arrived.

Finally, she could delay no longer. Her name was called. The time had come for her to give him her hand. Slowly she stepped forward as he approached. She raised her head and their eyes met.

The prince was her servant! The servant was her prince! He had traveled with her to make sure that she would be safe and cared for. This was the man she had learned to love. Overwhelmed with relief and joy, she gladly walked into his waiting arms. And as all good stories end, they lived happily ever after.

This old legend shouts some basic truths—of the power of humility and of putting others first. But Jesus Christ, our Elder Brother, went far beyond what we in our humanity would consider necessary.

Christ came to this world as a servant, ministering to all. On the last evening of His life He knelt on the floor and washed the travel-stained feet of His disciples. He held in His hands the feet of Judas, washing them with tenderness. Incredible!

But someday He will return as King of kings and Lord of lords, and "every knee will bow and every tongue confess" that Jesus Christ is King.

Rodney Griffin's song based on our Scripture takes us to the upper room. He says that he loves to write songs in the first person. He tries to put himself in someone else's shoes, to try to feel what they were feeling at a particular moment. Judas was the one, in the upper room that night, with the hidden agenda.

"But," Rodney says, "while others that night were enthralled with the words of the Master, Judas was hearing the clang of 30 silver coins. That was until Jesus masterfully confronted him. As only a holy, humble servant would, Jesus prepared a basin of water, girded Himself with a towel, and one by one washed the disciples' feet. His goal … Judas.

"He and Judas were the only ones in the room who knew what was going on behind the scenes. It was classic darkness versus light. How would Jesus react to the one He knew would in a few minutes betray Him? Would He embarrass Judas by telling of the secret sin that was lodged in his heart and then refuse to wash his feet because of it? I've often wondered what went through Judas' mind at that moment. Knowing he deserved scolding for what he was plotting, he watched Jesus with cautious eyes. Finally the moment of truth came … the most awkward moment in history. Purity knelt before the pathetic. Holiness knelt before hatred … and served him. Jesus carefully and lovingly washed the feet of the one who would soon lead Him to an old rugged cross."

Rodney continues, "Why did I write this song? What motivated me? If I were honest with you, I would tell you that it's because Judas and I have a lot in common. We've both dropped the ball when we should have carried it further. We've both turned our heads when someone needed us. We've both been portrayed to be something we are not. But thanks be to God, we have one more thing in common—we've both had our feet washed by a precious loving and forgiving Master, Who said, 'I love you, anyway.'"

He Washed My Feet

"The moment our eyes met, I knew this was the night,
That I would betray Him, the precious Lamb of God.
No other disciple was aware of my plan,

Till He rose from the table with something in His hand.
His holy eyes pierced through me, revealing all my sin
I knew His wrath was coming, and this would be the end.

"But He bowed, and He washed my feet,
Knowing that I was the cause of His grief;
When He should have scolded, He whispered 'Peace,'
As He bowed, and He washed my feet.

"Judas would fail Him, but he's no worse than I
The moment I gave in to Satan's compromise,
Ungrateful that Jesus had saved me from hell,
I was walking too proudly and that's when I fell.
His holy eyes pierced through me, revealing all my sin,
I knew His wrath was coming, and this would be the end.

"But He bowed, and He washed my feet,
Knowing that I was the cause of His grief;
When He should have scolded, He whispered, 'Peace,'
As He bowed, and He washed my feet."

(Words and Music by Rodney Griffin)

"Then a Samaritan, a race of people who are hated by the Jews, came along the road. When he saw the man, he felt sorry for him, even though he could tell that he was a Jew.

"He soothed his wounds with a salve made from oil and wine. Then he helped the man get up, mounted him on his donkey and took him to the nearest inn on the outskirts of Jericho where he cared for him all through the night.

"The next morning before he left, he gave the manager of the place the equivalent of two days' wages and said, 'I'd like for you to take care of this man until he's well enough to go on. If it costs more than this, I'll pay the difference when I stop here next time.'"

(LUKE 10:33-35, *The Clear Word*)

Chapter 15

Samaritan's Heart

"Did you know that you make over 2,500 choices every day?
The quality of your life is determined by your decisions."

(Joel Osteen)

"Twenty years ago, I drove a cab for a living. When I arrived for my first fare at 2:30 A.M. on this particular morning, the building was dark except for a single light in a ground floor window. Under these circumstances, many drivers would just honk once or twice, wait a minute, and then drive away.

"But I had seen too many impoverished people who depended on taxis as their only means of transportation. Unless a situation smelled of danger, I always went to the door. '*This passenger might be someone who needs my assistance,*' I reasoned to myself.

"So I walked to the door and knocked. 'Just a minute,' answered a frail, elderly voice. I could hear something being dragged across the floor.

"After a long pause, the door opened. A small woman in her 80s stood before me. She was wearing a print dress and a pillbox hat with a veil pinned on it, like somebody out of a 1940s movie. By her side was a small nylon suitcase. The apartment looked as if no one had lived in it for years. All the furniture was covered with sheets.

"There were no clocks on the walls, no knickknacks or utensils on the counters. In the corner was a cardboard box filled with photos and glassware.

"'Would you carry my bag out to the car?' she asked. I took the suitcase to the cab, and then returned to assist the woman.

"She took my arm and we walked slowly toward the curb. She kept thanking me for my kindness.

"'It's nothing,' I told her. 'I just try to treat my passengers the way I would want my mother treated.'

"'Oh, you're such a good boy,' she said.

"When we got in the cab, she gave me an address, then asked, 'Could you drive through downtown?'

"'It's not the shortest way,' I answered quickly.

"'Oh, I don't mind,' she said. 'I'm in no hurry. I'm on my way to a hospice.' I looked in the rearview mirror. Her eyes were glistening. 'I don't have any family left,' she continued. 'The doctor says I don't have very long.'

"I quietly reached over and shut off the meter. 'What route would you like me to take?' I asked.

"For the next two hours, we drove through the city. She showed me the building where she had once worked as an elevator operator. We drove through the neighborhood where she and her husband had lived when they were newlyweds. She had me pull up in front of a furniture warehouse that had once been a ballroom where she had gone dancing as a girl.

"Sometimes she'd ask me to slow down in front of a particular building or corner and would sit staring into the darkness, saying nothing.

"At the first hint of sun creasing the horizon, she suddenly said, 'I'm tired. Let's go now.'

"We drove in silence to the address she had given me. It was a low building, like a small convalescent home, with a driveway that passed under a portico.

"Two orderlies came out to the cab as soon as we pulled up. They were solicitous and intent, watching her every move. They must have been expecting her.

"I opened the trunk and took the small suitcase to the door. The woman was already seated in a wheelchair.

" 'How much do I owe you?' she asked, reaching into her purse.

" 'Nothing,' I said.

"'You have to make a living,' she answered.

"Almost without thinking, I bent and gave her a hug. She held onto me tightly.

" 'You gave an old woman a little moment of joy,' she said. 'Thank you.'

"I squeezed her hand, then walked into the dim morning light. Behind me a door shut. It was the sound of the closing of a life. I didn't pick up any more passengers that shift. I drove aimlessly, lost in thought. For the rest of that day, I could hardly talk.

"*What if that woman had gotten an angry driver, or one who was impatient to end his shift?*

"*What if I had refused to take the run, or had honked once, and then driven away?*

"On a quick review, I don't think that I have done anything more important in my life. We're conditioned to think that our lives revolve around great moments. But the great moments often catch us unaware—beautifully wrapped in what others may consider a small one."

A wise friend once told me, "*People may not remember exactly what you did, or what you said, but they will always remember how you make them feel.*"

Someone has said, "Life is not a journey to the grave with the intention of arriving safely in a pretty and well preserved body, but rather to skid in broadside, thoroughly used up, totally worn out, and loudly proclaiming, 'Wow, what a ride!'"

God's favor and blessing are on His children who are available to do His work of encouragement, His work of loving. Mother Teresa once wrote, "Life is not made up of extraordinary works, but of little things done with extraordinary love." These are our daily choices, and because of His presence, all things are possible. I want to remember to invest my life making a difference in the lives of others, and not only to sing but also to put a song in someone else's heart today.

Rodney's and Gerald Crabb's song voices the heart-longing of every child of God.

Samaritan's Heart

"One day a traveler journeyed down the road to Jericho,
He was beaten by some thieves and left to die.
Teachers of religion and the law came near to where he lay,
But the Levite and the Priest just passed him by.

"He wondered if the God they served had a heart of stone,
Does He walk on by whenever we're in pain?
All at once he saw a stranger reaching out with love and kindness,
Who healed his wounds and put him on the right way.

"He didn't need the law that would teach him right from wrong and how he'd sinned,
Religion couldn't help him mend the shattered, broken pieces back again.
He was hoping for one person who would open up their heart and take the time,
Lord grant that I would show Your light and that Samaritan's heart would be mine.

"I too was like that traveler who walked down the road of sin,
Wounded by the thief and left to die,
I tried religion and the law but couldn't find my way,
It seemed that help would always pass me by.

"Would the choices that I made in life curse my soul forever?
Could God forgive me of my past mistakes?
All at once I saw a nail-scarred hand reach out in love and kindness,
He healed my wounds and put me on the right way.

"I didn't need the law that would teach me right from wrong and how I'd sinned,
Religion couldn't help me mend the shattered, broken pieces back again.
I was hoping for one Person who would open up their heart and take the time,
Just like that Samaritan, Lord, I thank You that You did not pass me by.

"There's a host of broken people lying by the dusty road,

God's touch is what they're needing; it's up to us to lead them home.

Cause they don't need the law that would teach them right from wrong and how they'd sinned,

Religion will not help them mend the shattered, broken pieces back again.

"They just need one person who will open up their heart and take the time,

Lord grant that I would show Your light, and that Samaritan's heart would be mine."

Words and music by Rodney Griffin and Gerald Crabb

PHOTOGRAPHS

(From left) Bill West, Rodney Griffin, and Rodney's father, Jeff Griffin. Jeff came to know the Lord through Bill's kind and gentle witness while on the job at the Newport News shipyard. The story, "Common Garments," can be found in Chapter 8.

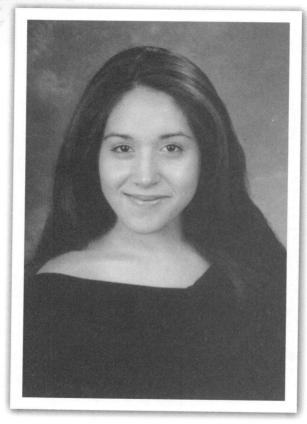

Janelle Jordana Solari miraculously shared a rose with a young man dying of a brain tumor in Chapter 9, "Let My Life Make a Difference." She is now studying to be a chaplain at Florida Hospital in Orlando.

The David Ring family: (front row) Amy Joy, Karen, and David; (back row) April, Nathan, and Ashley. Read David's inspiring story of triumph over adversity in Chapter 4, "God Wants to Hear You Sing–2."

*Charles Haugabrooks' story of singing through
grief is shared in Chapter 13, "My Name Is Lazarus."*

Mark Lodenkamp (center), is pictured here with his family before he died of a brain tumor. Through his connection with God, he was able to keep singing until the end. Today his family continues singing as they look forward to their reunion in heaven.
Read his remarkable story in Chapter 2, "More Than Able."

*You'll be touched by Beth Burden's story in Chapter 1, "God Wants to Hear You Sing–1."
The Burden family surrounded Beth (center) with love, prayer and music, as she fought
for her life against a tumor in her stomach.*

Teri and Tedd Webster with their children today, share their story of triumph after the tragedy of loss in Chapter 12, "No Valley."

Since organizing in 1990, Greater Vision has been delighting audiences with their rich vocal blend and their effective ability to communicate the message of the gospel.

The vocals and rich harmony for which Greater Vision has become recognized are a result of the blending of three unique and versatile vocalists. Rodney Griffin (left) is the prolific song writer of the group and handles the baritone part. Gerald Wolfe (center), the trio's founder and emcee, sings the lead. Jacob Kitson, the newest member, provides the exceptional tenor part.

"'I already know the plans I have for you.

I will help you, not hurt you.

I will give you a future and a hope.'"

(JEREMIAH 29:11, *The Clear Word*)

EPILOGUE:

After Worship, what's next?

WORSHIP CHANGES US. It's a heart-expanding experience. Any time we come into God's presence and are privileged to peer into His heart, we are compelled to get involved in what He is up to…we are moved to look around and discover what God is doing, and then join Him. When our hearts touch His, His burden becomes ours, His passion becomes part of us.

So, right now He may be wanting to show you something more about His great plans for your life, His big purpose for you that may totally dwarf any ideas you've ever had. He can take you to dramatic make-a-difference levels of service you've never dreamed of. Or it may be reaching out to someone right next door.

Fresh from your praise and worship you may find Him leading you to someone He loves, someone who needs Him. Look around and ask Him who He wants you to bless today.

We are never closer to the heart of God than when we have reported for service. He often asks us to do simple things. Like sitting with a couple of kids so their harried mother can have a few minutes for herself. Standing at the bedside of one of God's senior citizens, maybe not even talking…just being there. Listening while a youngster practices his reading lesson. Or how about that shut-in you've been missing at church lately… When we intentionally look at others through God's eyes, He'll show us how He wants to love them through us.

I know, these are simple things, but our Father calls this real business, Kingdom Business. He wants us to join Him in loving His world because He knows that this kind of active caring not only brings a smile to the hearts of others, but what could be more ennobling to us than to know that we are co-workers with the God who put the stars in place?

That's why John Bunyan, author of "Pilgrim's Progress," could write: "You haven't lived today until you have done something for someone who cannot pay you back."

It's true: If you want your life to take on new meaning, get involved in something bigger than your own circumstances.

What kinds of things are going on where you are? What are the needs of the place where you live? At the end of this chapter, you'll find a list – just some suggestions – of organizations you can help which are making a difference – and they need you. You'll think of many others.

And a final word from Rodney: "Don't forget the needs of your own local church. There are many ways that you can 'lift the load' and make things move more smoothly – you can make it possible for your church to reach those who need hope. You're needed right there. As a wise preacher once told me, 'Your light should shine the brightest at home.'"

A few suggestions for ways to get involved – here's a start . . . you'll think of more:

U.S. Dream Academy Inc.

▸ is an organization dedicated to making America a better place by starting with the most significant members of society – our children.

▸ for thousands of young people – an absent father, an addicted mother, a guardian, brother, aunt, uncle or neighbor in jail is not the exception but the rule.

▸ by giving youth education, encouragement, and confidence, we can provide them with hope and opportunity they need to become great achievers.

You can volunteer to be a mentor, or help financially

Contact:

US Dream Academy, 10400 Little Patuxent Parkway, Suite 300, Columbia, Maryland 21044
Phone: 1-800-USDREAM | www.usdreamacademy.org

Feed The Children — Making a Difference Today

▸ helps to feed hungry children around the world, in the United States, and works with abandoned babies.

You can help –
      Send a donation now
      Go on a mission
      Become a special project fundraiser
      Help a child succeed in school
      Support disaster relief

Contact:

Feed The Children, PO Box 36, Oklahoma City, OK 73101-0036
Phone- 1-800-627-4556 | www.feedthechildren.org

SAMARITAN'S PURSE INTERNATIONAL

▸ is a non-denominational Christian international relief agency -

▸ meeting the physical needs of victims of war, natural disaster and disease with the aim of demonstrating God's love.

▸ find out how much difference a shoe box can make with Operation Christmas Child

▸ World Medical Missions – and much more.

CONTACT:
Samaritan's Purse, PO Box 3000, Boone, NC 28607
Phone: 828-262-1980 | www.samaritanspurse.org

IN TOUCH MINISTRIES -

▸ Dr. Charles Stanley (who often partners with Greater Vision) offers several online resources through the ministry's Web site, InTouch.org.

▸ Read and hear daily devotionals, listen to his daily radio program, and watch In Touch's weekly television broadcast.

▸ You can also find information on cruises with Dr. Stanley and other special In Touch events.

▸ Shop at In Touch's online bookstore, make a donation, or check out career opportunities with the ministry.

CONTACT:
In Touch Ministries, P.O. Box 7900, Atlanta, GA 30357
Phone: 1-800-789-1473 | www.intouch.org

Compassion International

‣ is one of the nation's largest Christian child sponsorship organizations, working with more than 65 denominations and thousands of indigenous church partners around the world.

‣ sponsor a child

Contact:

Compassion International, 12290 Voyager Parkway, Colorado Springs, CO 80921
Phone: 1-800-336-7676 | www.compassion.org

ADRA International

‣ The Adventist Development and Relief Agency (ADRA) was initiated by the Seventh-day Adventist Church to follow Christ's example by partnering with those in need.

‣ ADRA seeks to identify and address social injustice and deprivation in developing countries.

‣ The agency's work seeks to improve the quality of life of those in need. ADRA invests in the potential of those individuals through community development initiatives targeting Food Security, Economic Development, Primary Health and Basic Education. ADRA's emergency management initiatives provide aid to disaster survivors.

‣ ADRA's ministry is dependent to a large extent, on private donations from faithful partners. Make your donations and support ADRA wherever the needs are currently the greatest.

‣ These donations develop entire communities, making life worth living for almost 24 million people worldwide.

Contact:

ADRA International, 12501 Old Columbia Pike, Silver Spring, MD 20904
Phone: 1-800-424-2372 | www.adra.org

OTHER BOOKS BY THE JACOBSENS:

By Ruthie Jacobsen:

Do It The Right Way

A Passion For Prayer (co-authored with Lonnie Melashenko & Tim Crosby)

The Difference Is Prayer

Kneeling On the Promises

Because You Prayed (co-authored with Penny Estes Wheeler)

Prayer, A Still Place In the Storm

Putting Their Hands In His, Teaching Children To Pray

By Don Jacobsen:

Call to Joy

The authors may be contacted at:

ruthiej@earthlink.net

or

1donj@earthlink.net